COMPACT CYMRU

CW01510338

n

A History of Trawstynydd Artillery Camp

Keith T. O'Brien

Gwasg Carreg Gwalch

First published in 2021
© Keith T. O'Brien / Gwasg Carreg Gwalch
© photographs: Keith T. O'Brien

ISBN: 978–1-84524-341-8

Cover design: Eleri Owen

Published by Gwasg Carreg Gwalch,
12 Iard yr Orsaf, Llanrwst, Wales LL26 0EH
tel: 01492 642031
email: books@carreg-gwalch.cymru
website: www.carreg-gwalch.cymru

This book is dedicated to the memory of my late Father, John "O'B" O'Brien who came to Traws Camp to do his national service with No 1 EDU (Explosives Demolition Unit) of the Royal Army Ordnance Corps in the early 50s, before marrying and settling in Traws for the rest of his life.

KEITH O'BRIEN

A native of Trawsfynydd in Gwynedd, married and has two daughters. He is a Member of Trawsfynydd Community Council since 1995, a Chairman of Traws-Newid community company since its incorporation in 1998. Traws-Newid is responsible for developing the environmental, economic and social aspects of Trawsfynydd. He is also chair on the Friends of Yr Ysgwrn, a group of volunteers who contribute to the aims and objectives of the Yr Ysgwrn project (Hedd Wyn's home), which is now managed by Snowdonia National Park Authority.

Work In 2004 he accepted a post with the Snowdonia National Park Authority as Sustainability and Community Officer, following several posts in the technical department of the former Meirionnydd District Council and Gwynedd Council.

Photography He has a few interests, such as local history, walking and cycling but without doubt photography is his main interest. He does not limit himself to one style but enjoys taking all forms of photography, especially landscapes, astrophotography (which has been a useful contribution to the Park's accreditation as a dark sky reserve). As well as wildlife – he considers himself extremely fortunate to live in an area brimming with rare species.

His photographs can be found on the following website: http://www.pbase.com/gefailgof

Contents

Introduction   4

Part 1
Antiquities   8
   Bedd Porius (Porius' Grave)   10
   Rhiwgoch   16
   Penstryd Stone Circle   34
   Llech Idris   38
   The Feidiog Isa' Tragedy   40
   Before the Soldiers Arrived   48

Part 2   49
Introduction   50
   The Land – From South Africa to
     Cwm Dolgain   54
   Transport Problems   60
   Social   70
   Balloon   80
   More Land Needed   92
   Clearing the Ranges   120

Acknowledgements   136
Bibliography   137

John O'Brien, the author's father in the middle

Page 1 photo: Rhiwgoch – Officers' Mess

Introduction

For the visitor the Trawsfynydd area appears as a mountainous and bleak space surrounded by rugged crags, yet in the midst of the open and desolate hills, wooded valleys exist full of birds and wildlife with meandering streams teaming with trout. A place to create a powerful impression on an individual's mind, a place, which very soon, manifests itself as one of the most beautiful locations in Wales, a place full of romance to inspire the poet and artist – a place that is scattered with the history of the past, as witnessed by its ancient monuments, a large number of which can be discovered in Cwm Dolgain, which is the subject area of this book.

The first thing you notice is the tranquillity and quiet of Cwm Dolgain, or the "Ranges" as it is known colloquially,

Bluebells and Dolgain
Dôl Moch sheepfold

Danger Farm

Danger Farm

which starts at Gallt y Darren and ends in Pistyll Cain with the river cascading down the one hundred and fifty feet high falls to join the Mawddach River. A romantic, wooded valley full of mountain bikers in its lower part, with exposed high mountain pastures in the upper part, where the sheep are more numerous than the cyclists and the buzzards dominate the skies rather than the jays.

Up until the end of the fifties of the last century, red flags were seen flying on the hill tops and the sound of big guns could be heard firing with their shells whistling through the air before burying themselves in the moorland peat of Dol Moch, Bryn-Pierce and Harry Howel, not far from Danger Farm, or Feidiog Isa' to give it its proper name.

A place that became home to a military camp and huge firing range that was a prominent artillery training ground for the British Army for almost 60 years. The site was used as one of only two artillery ranges to pilot field telephone systems, something that proved not only essential in terms of communication in order to gain ground in the First World War but also in saving lives.

It was this backdrop that prompted me to undertake research, collect old photos, and make general enquiries about twelve years ago in order to establish a more permanent record of the Camp. I proceeded throughout 2007 taking photos and identifying the locations of the military remains before they completely disappeared from the landscape. Incidentally, as a result of that exercise, Snowdonia National Park Authority saw fit to restore the dilapidated Llechweddgain observatory. An observatory with a view of the whole firing range, indeed a structure with a special feature to it, a masonry canopy not found on the other observatories.

During this time, I also recorded in and around Cwm Dolgain, 14 Splinter Proof Shelters; 3 Observatories; 22 Field Telephone Boxes; 1 Bunker; 1 Sentry Box and 8 Flag Bases.

For me it was all a labour of love, so I greatly appreciate Gwasg Carreg Gwalch's willingness to incorporate all the information that I gathered into this fine-looking and informative volume, without their assistance and patience the book would not have been possible.

Part 1

Before addressing the Camp and the Ranges, I intend to give an insight into the area's history firstly, so that the reader can appreciate the wealth of antiquities that belong to these special acres and thus provide an overall context to the subject matter.

Antiquities

Before the British Army occupied the land in the beginning of the twentieth century, soldiers' boots had marched across the land for some centuries before. The earliest example we are aware of is the Romans, since the old Roman Road, called Sarn Helen, passes close to the location and they had indeed set up a clay kiln (OS 728319) not far from Penstryd, for the purpose of making pottery and roofing tiles for the Roman fort of Tomen y Mur, which is on the northern boundary of the Parish.

Then there is the story of Cromwell's Roundheads in the vicinity in the 17th century persecuting captain John Morgan of Gelli Iorwerth (Plas Capten) because he was loyal to the King. Legend has it that he was shot dead by them at the cave of Carreg yr Ogof, which used to be on the shore of Traws Lake.

We will now turn our attention to the most prominent places and their history.

Roman clay kiln near Penstryd

Range warning sign

Bedd Porius (Porius' Grave)

Bedd Porius (OS 733313) is situated a few yards to the east of the road that leads down to Bont Dol y Mynach in Cwm Dolgain. Maes y Bedd (Grave Field) is the name of the field where the grave lies but is this the correct location? Indeed, this is one of the mysteries connected with the site as we will discover below.

6th Century Stone

The gravestone on the site today is a replica of the original. Well to be honest there are two replicas with the head of one at the foot of the other. Denise Angster was the sculptor responsible for making the copies as the original stone was taken to the National Museum of Wales in Cardiff in 1933. The copies were formed in concrete which are now in very poor condition, with the concrete cracking and moss growing over them. Some years ago it was decided to change one of the copies for a more recent one in better condition, but despite the efforts of a muscular crew it was impossible to shift the original copy so it was left in place with the other at its feet. The grave is surrounded by a low wall of slate laid on edge, with iron railings outside it. When the army used the land in the first half of the last century, there was also a cast iron star on a post nearby to warn the soldiers to keep clear of it whilst on exercises. The dimensions of the stone are three foot and four inches by two foot by four inches with a thickness of eight inches. The lowest corner has broken off. The stone is thought to date back to the late 5th century or early 6th century.

A number of antiquarians have visited the site over the centuries, with none other than Edward Llwyd himself making the first record around 1698, where he describes the stone as lying within two fields of Llech Idris and with the following lettering on it: PORIVS / HIC IN TVMVLO IACIT / HOMO ¨ ¯PIANVS FVIT – Here lies Porius in the grave. He was a Christian person.

In 1742 Lewis Morris visited the site and, a little later, Thomas Pennant too. They wrote the words down exactly as Edward Llwyd had done. In 1846 Longville Jones took a rubbing of the stone that once again confirmed the wording that was noted previously. But by 1884 when Archdeacon Thomas visited the site, he noticed that 'PLANVS' and not 'PIANVS' was written in the last line – as it is today.

Therefore, it is obvious that the letter 'I' was changed to the letter 'L' sometime between 1846 and 1884. This mystery has been a talking point for many antiquarians over the years and it is likely that the most sensible answer is the following one.

On the face of it the word PIANVS doesn't mean anything in Latin and it is likely that someone felt they would be doing a big favour by adding a 'foot' to the 'I' changing it to 'L', as PLANVS is a Latin word (but it doesn't make any sense in this context). In order to make sense one must look at the gap between the 'O' and the 'P' in 'HOMO ¨ ⁻PIANVS'. If we can accept the letter 'X' had been in the gap with the hyphen connecting it to the 'P', and that the 'P' represents rho from the Greek chi-rho, then it would recreate as 'X~P~IANUS'. This makes a lot more sense

as He was a Christian person, rather than He was a plain person.

So, what happened to the letter 'X' (or maybe +)? It is possible that it was removed in the Puritanical Cromwell age. It was a practice of some of the most extreme religious persuasion of the time to destroy any ancient carved monuments because they included, in their opinion, the devil's language – Latin. An 'X' or '+' of course was a Christian symbol and therefore it is quite possible to believe it was erased from the stone.

Before leaving the wording,

underneath the letters referred to above, are the following figures, 1245 E. Unfortunately, no information is available about these, only that they are not contemporary with the main text.

Sadly, as we will see, it is not completely clear where exactly the location of the original grave is and because of that the site cannot be considered as a scheduled ancient monument.

When Pennant visited the site in 1773, he noted that the stone lay freely on top of some sort of grave near a farmhouse by the road to Rhiwgoch. Pennant's description is fairly vague, but we then have more definite information from Longueville Jones' visit in 1846 where he notes a few years earlier that W.W.E. Wynne of Peniarth called to see the stone only to find that the farmer was building it into a wall. W.W.E. Wynne informed Sir Watkin Williams Wynn, the owner of Llech Idris Farm about the incident and as a result Sir Robert Williams Vaughan, Nannau arranged, on behalf of the Wynnstay Estate, for the stone to be protected in a small enclosure. According to local tradition the enclosure is about fifty yards in front of the place designated as Maes y Bedd (Grave Field), namely the original site of the grave.

Hemp and Gresham suggest in Archaeolegia Cambrensis, 110, 1961 that the grave is Roman, and that it is sited near Sarn Helen in accordance with the tradition of burying eminent Roman remains by the roadside.

However, if the extent of Cymmer Abbey land is considered, which stretched up to Cwm Dolgain and included the vast part of Moel Llyfnant, Moel y Feidiog, Mynydd Bryn-llech and Mynydd Bach and almost up to Cefndeuddwr; and then consider the old farm names Dol y Mynach Isaf (Lower Monk's Meadow) and Dol y Mynach Uchaf (Upper Monk's Meadow) – which is opposite Maes y Bedd, we get a different slant on the matter.

Llywelyn the Great included a place called Bedd yr Esgob (Bishop's Grave) in his charter to the monks of Cymer in 1209. The description of the place is detailed enough for it to be placed on the eastern bank of Afon Cain opposite but a little higher up than the present site of Bedd Porius. A number of historians have suggested that this is more than a coincidence and that it is possible that

Bedd Porius and Bedd yr Esgob are the same place. This would, of course, fit in well with the theory of the lost sign from the stone – the chi-rho; indeed, it would date sensibly to the 6th century, the age of Saints – when numerous Bishops existed in Wales.

Porius' Grave

Over:
Crescent moons of Feidiog Isa's Irish Bridge

Rhiwgoch

This is the ancient home of the Llwyd (Lloyd) family whose genealogy stretches back to Llywarch ap Brân, Lord of Menai, founder of the second of the Fifteen Noble Tribes of Wales, who lived on Anglesey during the twelfth century. The Latin family motto was *Sequere justitiam et invenias vitam* – Follow justice and discover life. We will discuss the important people connected with this building later, but firstly we'll take a detailed look at the buildings and their special attributes.

Gatehouse

In order to gain a sense and appreciation of the site, we will begin our journey by standing in the yard between the bungalow and the gatehouse as this was the proper entrance to the manor, a Crown Manor, as we shall see. The first thing we notice are the cobbles under foot, every stone set tidily next to each other in a pattern that leads us towards the gatehouse entrance.

Before going through the entrance we turn to the west to glance at the mansion's stable. The stable is thought to date back to the 18th or early 19th century, and like the mansion and gatehouse the stable is a grade II listed building; built in stone with a slate roof. Two casement windows are to the right of the door and one to the left. There is a stable loft up above and entrance to it is gained by climbing external stone steps on the southern gable end. There is another window on the western elevation.

Back to the gatehouse. Before going through the entrance, we see above the lintel the Lloyd's motto with their coat of arms carved in stone and inserted into the wall. As explained above the motto is Sequere justitiam et invenias vitam. The coat of arms is described as 'Silver, between three crows with ermine in beaks and a black chevron' which is the coat of arms of Llywarch ap Brân. The building is around 15 feet wide with an obvious join to the left where it was extended later to create a cowshed.

1. Sketch of Rhiwgoch circa 1857;
2. Motto above gatehouse entrance;
3. Rhiwgoch gatehouse

Walking through the gatehouse we arrive at a quadrangle measuring 30 by 27 feet and what an interesting place! Turing on our heels to face the gatehouse from the other side, above the lintel here carved in stone we see the Royal Arms of the Tudor Family, which include a lion and dragon supporting a shield with a crown on top of it (the Stewarts were responsible for replacing the Welsh dragon with the unicorn). This sign confirms the importance of Rhiwgoch as a Crown Manor, namely a place where royalty would stay when in the area. There is a row of stone steps to the right of the entrance which lead to the upper floor, which was a café at the end of the eighties of the last century.

Bee Hives

To the left of the gatehouse four huge slate shelves can been seen connecting the gatehouse with the mansion house. According to local tradition these were a place where the bodies of criminals would lie after they were hanged from the protruding stone which is halfway between the first-floor windows nearby. Of course, this tale is complete nonsense because their purpose was nothing more than shelves to hold skeps (beehives). In the old days sugar was very scarce, especially in remote places such as Rhiwgoch, so it was usual to keep skeps for the bees to have honey as a sweetener instead of sugar. This sort of shelter was fairly common in windy and rainy places and as in this example they all faced south so that the early morning sun could warm the bees. Of course, this doesn't explain why the stone protrusion is there; looking at an old photograph of the mansion house dating back to 1905, with a little bit of effort, it can be seen in the same place. Who knows what its purpose was: Perhaps it was a perch for pigeons, because a little to the right of the northern window there are closed-up pigeonholes – this feature is obvious in the 1905 picture. There was also another pigeonhole in the gatehouse to the right of the door at the top of the stone steps where the small window is now. Looking carefully at the window to the left of the door, solitary stones can be seen set each side of the opening and they too jut out of the building – but they are not as obvious as the protrusion on the main building. As a matter of interest, until the arrival of root crops it was not possible to produce enough feed to keep the animals through the winter, so they had to be killed and salted to preserve them. So, the only source of fresh meat available during the winter and early spring months were the pigeons. Thousands upon thousands were bred for that purpose throughout the land by the gentry between the 13th and 18th century.

Second Lieutenant Frank Harry Turner circa 1920's

Ancient Door

Walking on along the cobbled path the front door is soon reached. The antiquity of the door and its opening is obvious from the date carved to the right of the sandstone frame, 1610. This type of entrance is described as a four centred arch. To the left are the letters R ^{M} Ll for Margaret and Robert Lloyd. To the right of the doorbell is the name Owen Owen and the date 1739. Above the arch is a shield with a helmet and a crow on top in sandstone relief. The effects of weathering and time have obliterated the coat of arms from the centre of the shield. For information, the arms were recorded by Lewys Dwnn as part of his work 'Heraldic Visitations' on the 25 July 1588 and a fee of 5 shillings was paid to him by Robert Lloyd. The door is made of solid oak with a studded surface. By stepping back, it can be seen that this part of the mansion is finished in dressed stone; whilst the other part, where the bar and the lounge used to be, is built of random rubble and belongs to an earlier period, perhaps the 12th century.

Prince of Wales' Bedroom

The front door opens into a hall which was finished in oak in the style of plank and muntin. Near to the door, a chamfered braced arched beam with a chamfered side post. Leading from the hall is a staircase and, halfway up, a door leading outside. The staircase then turns back on itself before rising to the top of the flight. At the top of the stairs is a door to the left leading into a very important room.

We are now in the bedroom of Prince Henry, the eldest son of James I. Henry stayed at Rhiwgoch whilst on a journey through Wales in 1610, and that is why that

Henricus Princeps initials – Prince Henry from 1610

year is noted on the frame of the front door in dedication to him. But there is another special tribute to him in the bedroom where it is likely that he slept because the fireplace is also dedicated to him. The plaster moulding (made during the 30s of the last century) above the fireplace takes the place of the original carved stone, but it is claimed that it faithfully follows the pattern of the carved stone. Two small pilasters can be seen

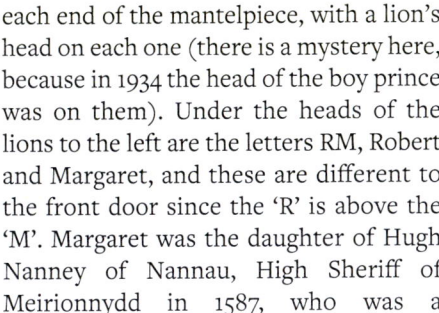

1. Fireplace in Prince Henry's bedroom;
2. Fireplace sketch by Major R.P. Waller in 1934

each end of the mantelpiece, with a lion's head on each one (there is a mystery here, because in 1934 the head of the boy prince was on them). Under the heads of the lions to the left are the letters RM, Robert and Margaret, and these are different to the front door since the 'R' is above the 'M'. Margaret was the daughter of Hugh Nanney of Nannau, High Sheriff of Meirionnydd in 1587, who was a descendant of the founder of the Third Royal Tribe of Wales. It is argued by some that that is why the 'M' is above the 'R' on the front door, because her 'Royal' Tribe ancestry has a higher status than the 'Noble' Tribe of her husband!

On a pilaster to the right of the mantelpiece are the letters 'Ll' for Lloyd, of course. Between the pilasters are the Prince of Wales feathers with a helmet around them and the capital letters 'H' and 'P' either side of the helmet Henricus Princeps, Prince Henry. The sun's rays dance around it; and beyond to the left is a rose and to the right a thistle.

Under the shelf, three shields are moulded into the plaster and when the mansion was a dining room for the army officers in the last century, the shelves held photographs of the Camp's Commandants. Long ago the coats of arms of the Lloyds, Nanneys and Ithel ap Iorwerth would probably have had pride of place on them.

Connected to the Prince's room was the ladies chamber. In here *Dutch* tiles were laid on the floor with scriptural signs upon them.

Expensive Wine!

Returning to the top of the stairs. There is a small room facing the north at the top of the stairs. This would have been a pantry originally, but it was changed to 'Expensive Wine Store' when the place was the Officer's Mess. When the mansion was in the ownership of Sir Watkin Wynn from the Wynnstay Estate, this was the main bedroom lined with oak panels throughout. Before Sir Watkin sold Rhiwgoch to the army in 1905, he removed the panels and installed them in the billiards room at Wynnstay, where they say they can still be seen today.

Hot Pikelets and the Trapdoor

In the old days there was a trapdoor in the floor of the main bedroom connected to the kitchen (where the toilets used to be), and there is an interesting little story connected to the trapdoor that is worth repeating:

The trapdoor's main purpose was for the lady of the house to be able to contact the maids quickly to quieten them if they made too much noise. Back in the 19th century a young boy (name not known unfortunately) used to sleep with his grandmother and grandfather near the trapdoor. The boy noted that he remembered in the morning hearing the maid knocking on the trapdoor before opening it slowly and, with the help of a toasting fork, pushing up a hot pikelet with butter melting over it for his pleasure eating it whilst sitting in his bed!

Hall

The manor house hall was where the lounge is now, namely the 'great hall', here the gentry would entertain their guests. Indeed, the Lloyds were noted as patrons of the bards. The joyful evenings there can only be imagined, by the huge fire that

used to burn where the serving bar used to be; red and yellow flames dancing up the chimney, the wood fire crackling in the heat and the bards singing the praises of their patrons.

Through into where the bar is today, there was another flight of stairs on the western side to go up to the bedrooms. On the northern side, where the fire is, there was a small Dutch parlour from the period of Charles II. There was room for four in the parlour, the squire, his wife and two guests.

Extension

As seen above, Rhiwgoch has changed quite a bit in its design over the years. The windows on the ground floor belong to the original period, whilst those on the first floor belong to the period of Charles II. It may be that at one time the first floor was a gallery or a grand reception. Robert Lloyd built the extension in 1610, which is the eastern annex that includes the main entrance. But it was the army that was responsible for the changes that gave the immediate past form to the building.

After creating the Officer's Mess in 1905, a large extension was built to the right in 1939. It is now the dining room with a connecting kitchen parallel to the 1610 extension. Between these two extensions a beer cellar was added in the middle of the nineteen eighties.

Rhiwgoch Gentry

The Lloyds of Rhiwgoch have already been mentioned. They were the owners of the manor house during the 15th, 16th and most of the 17th century. They were the descendants of Llywarch ap Brân. Llywarch was the brother in law of Owain Gwynedd, King of North Wales, because both had married two sisters. Griffith, the ninth descendant of the Llywarch line, married a second wife, Gwenhwyfar, daughter and heiress of Ithel ap Iorwerth, or to give him his full name, Ithel ap Iorwerth ap Einion ap Llewelyn ap Cynwrig ap Osborn Wyddel (from Corsygedol – where the same motto is carved as at Rhiwgoch, namely Sequere justitiam et invenias vitam). Gelli Iorwerth (Plas Capten), Trawsfynydd was the home of Ithel ap Iorwerth and Gwenhwyfar, but their son is described as William Lloyd of Rhiwgoch. The Lloyds were an important family in Meirionnydd and the great grandson of William, Robert Lloyd was the MP for Meirionnydd in 1586, 1601 and 1614, as well as being High Sheriff on four occasions.

The Saint and Martyr, John Roberts, was a cousin to Robert Lloyd, because Ellis,

Robert Lloyd's father, and Robert, the father of the Saint were two brothers. Saint John Roberts was born in Rhiwgoch in 1577. He made a great name for himself helping the sufferers of the Plague in London. Catholics have a special reverence for him, and he is regarded as a second Augustine because he was the first monk to return to England after Henry VIII's dissolution of the monasteries. He was also responsible for re-establishing and re-invigorating the Benedictine order in England. He was just thirty-three years old, the same age as Christ, when he was executed as punishment for high treason. The flame of the Old Faith was extinguished when his heart was thrown into the fire at Tyburn after he was hung,

1. *Saint John Roberts with repentant thief at Tyburn gallows; 2. Statue of Saint John Roberts at Downside Abbey near Bath*

drawn and quartered on the 10th December 1610. He was canonized as one of the Forty Martyrs of England and Wales on 25th October 1970 by Pope Paul VI (interestingly the 34 English martyrs were downgraded to a Feastday of the Blessed, whilst the 6 Welsh martyrs are still honoured with a Saints Day, which is 25th October).

Ellis, Robert Lloyd's son, followed his grandfather Hugh Nanney as High Sheriff in 1588 and once again in 1603. He died in 1616, years before his father.

Catherine, the daughter of Ellis, and the last of the Lloyd dynasty, inherited all the property. She married Henry Wynn, youngest son of Sir John Wynn of Gwydir. Henry was a bit of a pluralist as he held the positions of Protonotary of North Wales, Judge of Marshalsea, Steward of the Virge, Solicitor General to Queen Henrietta Maria and Secretary to the Court of the Marshes. He was the MP for Meirionnydd in the last Parliament of James I, as well as the first and fifteenth Parliament of Charles I. He died in 1671 – it's doubtful if Rhiwgoch saw much of him!

Henry's son was Sir John Wynn of Rhiwgoch. He was the Custos Rotulorum of Meirionnydd from 1707 to 1708. He was

the last baronet of the Gwydir Estate and it was Rhiwgoch's fate from that time on to fall into the occupation of the Wynnstay Estate. Sir John was a gardener and he created a small swan's egg pear tree, a pear tree that was very popular and named after him in 1799. Tradition has it that he developed the fruit in the gardens at Rhiwgoch.

John Garnons is the next to deserve our attention. He was a tenant of the Wynn's of Wynnstay. He was related through marriage to the Lloyds as he married Jane Roberts, granddaughter to Catherine Lloyd, sister of Robert Lloyd. He was a well-known solicitor in the county Sessions of Meirionnydd and Caernarfon. He employed several clerks in offices on the first floor of the building. He was High Sheriff of Caernarfonshire and Justice of the Peace for Meirionnydd. An interesting quotation comes from the diary of a woman called Elizabeth Barker in 1783, where she notes the following about sharing his will:

1. Rhiwgoch in 1905, prior to being converted to an Officers' Mess; 2. Rhiwgoch dining room; 3. Rhiwgoch stables and cowshed

Captain and Mrs Garnon with Miss Gwyn of Taliaris, the Rev. Parry and his wife are expected at Rhiwgoch next Thursday to share the personal property of the late Mr Garnon. According to Ellen Thomas' tea-table chat, who further said her late master had spent no less than £3,000 on Rhiwgoch, even though he was only a tenant. The land belonged to Sir Watkin Williams. Of course, his children now regret so large an expenditure upon the estate of another person who may not even thank them for it.

The next family to live at Rhiwgoch was the Roberts family (no relation to Saint John Roberts). One of them, David Roberts, contributed £400 to the Bible Society and as a result it was claimed that the act would bring great fame to the family and the parish 'whilst the water flowed'. This is the relevant part of his will dated 22nd September 1856:

> I give and bequeath to the 'British and Foreign Bible Society' instituted in London in the year 1804 the sum of four hundred pounds sterling ...

His brother was John Roberts and there is some mystery about this, as the following report from the *Dysgedydd*, August 1846 testifies:

> 11 June 1846 John Roberts, Rhiwgoch, Trawsfynydd died. This man had been away from home for over twenty years and none of his relatives knew what had become of him. They feared, as did others, that he had met with some unknown fatal accident.
>
> He used to go to England to sell cattle and it was there that he was lost. But much later, it was heard that he was ill in Cornwall. His two brothers went there and brought him home to the old country to his two sisters and one of his brothers, near Trawsfynydd church, where he died. He never married, and there was no dispute, that is known, between him and anyone in the family that caused his departure and remoteness towards them. He had also amassed great wealth and could have been as comfortable at home as anyone in the land.
>
> We heard that he was very fond of the companionship of religious men

after coming home and wanted them to pray for him – it was easy to admit he had lost his way by keeping himself from his family and that by doing so had caused such worry for them.

There is a plaque on the southern wall of St Madryn's Church recording the family as follows:

Saint Madryn's Church, Trawsfynydd

THE FAMILY OF RHIWGOCH

David Davies died 6th Dec 1781
Aged 24 years
Robert Roberts died 25 February 1787
Aged 12 years
Ann Davies died 20 March 1804
Aged 83 years
Robert Roberts died 21 January 1812
Aged 66 years
Jane wife of Robert Roberts died
July 14 1831. Aged 79 years

John Roberts died 11th June 1846
Aged 54 years
Jane Roberts died 14th February 1852
Aged 69 years
David Roberts died 19 June 1856
Aged 78 years
Elizabeth Roberts died 19th February
1860. Aged 74 years
Robert Roberts died 13th March 1871
Aged 80 years

After the Roberts family came the Pugh family. They were related to the Roberts as they were the grandchildren of Robert Roberts through the marriage of his daughter Eleanor Roberts to Hugh Pugh, Argoed, Harlech. They too were connected to the Lloyds and one of the oldest families in the area, very well respected and great contributors to the agricultural community. Robert Pugh was the father and he employed several maids and

Roberts' family plaque in St Madryn's Church

servants, an ostler and a cowman. He also employed up to 12 scythe-men in the hay cutting season. His son, Griffith, followed an apprenticeship as a carpenter and wheelwright in Oswestry and after finishing his time; he returned to Trawsfynydd and set up business there. Later he bought an oil engine with a generator and batteries to produce electricity for the village.

The late William Williams, Bryn Llefrith, addressed the Merionethshire Historical and Record Society in 1971, when they were on a site visit to Rhiwgoch. They were amazed when he showed them the horns of a bull that had been reared there. It needed a six foot wide door to go through it.

Thanks to Mr Bradshaw

To finish this part of the history of Rhiwgoch we take the opportunity to thank Mr Bradshaw. The idea of using the old manor house as a mess was considered by the sappers in Chester and it appears they stated they would have rather pulled it down or gut it internally and turn it into a storehouse. According to the correspondence in the Land Registry in Chester, the old mansion was not up to the required standards for a building belonging to the Government. Rhiwgoch was saved by a civilian Mr Bradshaw, who was employed by the office of the Principal Officer of the Royal Engineers. This gentleman undertook a survey of the site and concluded that the cost of repairing and converting the building would only cost £860 in comparison with the £1,600 needed for a corrugated iron mess, and it would be more comfortable. The report was final and because of it the old manor was saved. As Major R P Waller, M.C., R.A. said in 1934, 'Whether Mr Bradshaw is alive or not to receive our thanks, the Regiment has a debt of gratitude to him.' I think that the same thanks are due to him from the community of Trawsfynydd and to Major Waller also for recording the history of one of the oldest and most important manor houses in the area.

The army still used the place as an Officer's Mess up until 1956. At the end of the sixties the manor house was sold to the late Mrs Sally Snarr, Cross Foxes, Trawsfynydd. She then sold it on to the holiday village company around 1974, since then it has changed hands two or three times.

Fire

Sadly, to conclude this section, at about 12:30am on the 14th October, 2018, the Grade II Listed Building was gutted by fire following a fault on an electrical heating appliance. Six fire-fighting appliances, two water bowsers and an aerial ladder platform were used to fight the blaze. Firefighters spent more than 12 hours tackling the fire. Fortunately, nobody was injured, and firefighters prevented the fire spreading to nearby buildings.

1. Aerial view of Rhiwgoch after the fire; 2. Surveying the Damage; 3. Rhiwgoch fire; 4. Transferring Additional Water

Penstryd Stone Circle

Penstryd Stone Circle is probably the oldest monument in the area. The group of stones are situated on a mountain pasture 1,100 foot above sea level, approximately 300 yards south-west of Penstryd Chapel. Remnants of the circle can be found a few feet west of the road leading to Craig Penmaen.

There are six small sized stones with their tops cut off, making them difficult to spot in the rushes. Five of the stones are set in a circle with a diameter of 56 feet, with a gap of about 21 feet between them. The sixth stone is found just inside the circle radius, and if two other stones (perhaps missing) were placed 21 feet

either side of it, there would be a perfect circle of eight stones with a symmetrical effect.

The Beaker Folk began settling in Wales at around 1900BC and were responsible for erecting this kind of monument in Wales, i.e. a circle of standing stones. It is not clear what their purpose was, it is thought that they may have been for religious rituals, or some kind of elaborate grave. Whatever its purpose, it is important to the area because stone circles are not so numerous in Wales, as they are in other uplands.

Penstryd Stone Circle – three stones on the left and one on the right

Over:
Military road on the Feidiogydd

Llech Idris

Llech Idris is the most famous standing stone in Meirionnydd. It stands the length of two fields from Porius' grave to the south west. There isn't any definite information why the standing stones were erected but it is obvious that they were connected to the old prehistoric routes, with some of the routes having been in regular use right up to the 18th century.

Llech Idris and Maen Llwyd belong to a series of standing stones which start in the Llanbedr area (by virtue of the natural harbour of the river Artro to receive bronze products from the Wicklow area of Ireland). Then they lead behind Llandecwyn, through Cwm Moch to Cwm Dolgain, over to Bala and on to Montgomeryshire at the source of the Severn. From the source of the Severn the river can be followed to the Salisbury Plain and Thames Valley – the most important commercial and economic centres in Britain in the Bronze Age. It is most likely therefore, that they were way markers.

Llech Idris is a standing stone of solid sandstone. It measures 10½ feet in height by 5 feet in width with a depth of 12 inches.

The stone leans slightly to the east. When the army was training in the area during the last century, just as at Porius' grave, railings were erected around it with a cast iron star on a post nearby as a warning to keep away.

Chipping in a Shoe

The legend associated with the stone is connected to Idris the giant. According to the story, Idris was sitting on his chair, namely the mountain Cader Idris, when he felt something uncomfortable in his shoe which was causing him pain. He took his shoe off and found a chipping in it. In his temper he threw the chipping as far as he could – over to Cwm Dolgain and there it stands as Llech Idris!

Lord Idris

He is not to be confused with Idris the giant. Idris governed over the neighbourhood of Dolgellau and Llanelltyd in the 7th century. He was killed fighting against the Saxons somewhere in the Welshpool area in 632. His demise was so noteworthy that it is not only recorded

Llech Idris under the stars

in Annales Cambriae but also in the Irish Chronicles. Some are of the opinion that Llech Idris is a stone to note the territorial boundary of Lord Idris.

The Feidiog Isa' Tragedy

The soldiers called Feidiog Isa' 'Danger Farm'; it was just one of a number of smallholdings and farms that formed the agricultural community of Cwm Dolgain. Before the army took over the valley in 1903 these were the main dwellings, starting at the top end of the valley: Buarth Brwynog, Hafod y Garreg, Nant Lliwgys, Dol Moch Isaf, Dol Moch Uchaf, Feidiog Uchaf, Feidiog Ganol, Feidiog Isaf, Hafoty'r Plas (or Foty Llelo colloquially), Gelli Gain, Dôl Mynach Uchaf a Llech Idris.

An overwhelming sadness strikes one when thinking that the events of the outside world have led to the end of a way of life for the community of Cwm Dolgain, a remote and isolated valley, a valley full of life, laughter, blood, sweat and tears associated with the daily chores that were repeated from dawn to dusk like their forebears. Sadder still is the tale of Feidiog Isa' twenty-one years before the arrival of the army, when the place was shattered by a thunderbolt leaving two small children dead. This is the story:

Cruel Nature

November is not notable for good weather at best, a damp and misty month traditionally, but at half past one in the afternoon of the 8th November 1882 nature displayed its devastating and cruel side through a thunder and lightning storm of such ferocity that nobody could recall the likes of which ever before. So much was the fury of the storm that Edward Morris, the shepherd of Dol Moch, called in at Feidiog Isa' to shelter from the terrible weather. He was welcomed in by the head of the house, David Jones, who would have to face the greatest distress of his life in a few moments. His wife, Gwen, had gone on an errand to the village with her neighbour, Ann Williams, of Dol Mynach, and it was the first time she had left the house for months due to illness.

It was a house built with the chimney in the middle, a very effective way of sharing heat to all rooms. Apparently, at the time, David Jones and Edward Morris were by the gable end window, Lizzie, the daughter at a table opposite the front window, the two youngest boys by the fireplace and the other son was with his father. This is the scene in the harsh drama of nature, when, in a blink of an eyelid the chimney collapsed in smithereens down to the ground with the bedroom floors collapsing with it, burying the two youngest boys under a four and a half feet pile of rubble. Lizzie was thrown to the other side of the room with her arms and legs trapped in the debris and her head lay beside Edward Morris's dog which was dead by the dresser – but remarkably Lizzie was alive! Her ten-year-old brother, David, was also on the floor with severe burns on him. The neighbour, Edward Morris, was so traumatised that he could not concentrate or do anything – his hair, beard and his hands burned terribly. David Jones, the father, was fortunate to escape with his hair just lightly singed.

David Jones started clearing the rubble to free Lizzie immediately as she was crying ceaselessly and grieving from the loss of her other two brothers. Lizzie and David, the son, were placed in Edward Morris's care for him to take them to Dol Moch, the father afterwards tried desperately to get to the other two brothers. But the devastation was too much for one man to clear, so he had to leave and go and look for help to his neighbour, William Williams of Dol Mynach. Somehow, he managed to summon some great inner strength, despite his huge grief and anguish, to enable him to say what had happened to his neighbour.

'Are none of the family alive?'

William Williams gathered together three or four other neighbours to return to Feidiog Isa' in order to get to and release the children's bodies. At about the same

Feidiog Isa' converted into a field office by the army

Location of Feidiog Isa' behind Nant Ganol stream

time coming from Foty Llelo, on the other side of the valley, and fighting her way through the floods was Ellen Roberts. She had seen the destruction from afar and rushed there to help as soon as she could. She met the small crew from Dol Mynach not far from the house and noticed that not a single living soul was to be seen there, she asked worried and solemnly, 'Are none of the family alive?'

The apocalyptic damage was such that twenty-one years later it would be possible to forgive oneself for thinking that an enormous shell had struck the building. As they approached the house it was difficult to take stock of what they saw, trees and stones had been scattered up to two hundred yards away from the house, and sheep had been killed and were severely burned. The ground was scarred with furrows all over it running in all directions; the soil and the grass were scorched as well. The windows and doors had been shredded to pieces. Furniture, dishes and clothes were randomly mixed with the trees and stones in a manner resembling a scene from the Blitz.

Coli's Sacrifice

It took an hour and a half for three men to discover the children. They were under the impression that they had seen one of the children's hair when they realised that it was Coli the loyal and precious bitch. Coli lay across the chest and face of little five-and-a-half-year-old Morris, as if she had sacrificed her life to try to save him. The boy's body lay completely unscathed except for some minor burns to his ears and hair and his tiny hand was still clutching his toy archery bow.

After clearing a little more they found dear little Robert who was one and a half years old. The lightning's impression was imprinted deeply on his neck and his pretty little face.

The young bodies were carried to Dol Mynach, where the family were being cared for in their hour of need. G.J. Williams, Esq. the county coroner, held an inquest and the jury returned a verdict in accordance with the circumstances set out above.

They are buried at Penstryd Chapel cemetery; it's a simple enough gravestone without any mention of the tragedy on it. On the grave are the following words (in Welsh):

In Memory of
Morris son of David and Gwen
Jones Defidiog Isaf
Who died November 8th 1882
Aged 6 years old
Also Robert their son
Who died on the same day aged 1 year old

By their side is their mother's grave, Gwen, she died on the 23rd March 1891 at 54 years of age. Following her death, her husband, David, moved to Cae March, Llanfachreth. Feidiog Isa' was Siôn Ellis' home, Gwen's father, and it's mentioned that the house was built in 1857.

The Location Today

Unfortunately, there are no visible traces of Feidiog Isa' now to be found on the site mainly due to the efforts of the Forestry Commission in the nineteen seventies, when hundreds of trees were planted there. But, even if the remains of the building were there, was it the actual site of the Feidiog Isa' that was struck by lightning? It is quite easy to discover the site through the old military photos that exist – but, the 19th-century Ordnance Survey (OS) map shows its location to be about 300 yards to the south and on the west side of Nant Hir, not the east side! Perhaps the OS sometimes gets the names of our houses and streets wrong, but their maps are very reliable in terms of the accuracy of geographical features, even the old maps. So, was the Feidiog Isa' rebuilt after the lightning at a different site but with the same central-chimney feature?

I quote part of an article from the late William Williams Esq, Brynllefrith, which explains more about the individuals and their relations as follows:

Edward Morris the shepherd of Dol Moch was a native of Llanuwchllyn. He was the grandfather of Haf Morris, Dr Iwan Morris and the scientist Dewi Morris, B.A. Lizzie the saved daughter was the mother of the poet Morris Jones, Gyfannedd, Arthog (formerly) who married Kathi, Hedd Wyn's sister. Miss Williams who was with Gwen Jones when the disaster occurred was the mother of Martin Luther Jones, the last station master of Trawsfynydd. Today many of the descendants of Dafydd and Gwen Jones are highly respected in the Bala area as in Trawsfynydd; you only need to identify one and the rest will soon be found.

A son who was not home on the day of the disaster was Evan, the father of Ellen Roberts, the spouse of the late Tryweryn hero, Dafydd Roberts, Cae Fadog. The son saved by his father was of the same name as his, Dafydd Jones, Yr Ynys, Dyffryn, and he moved from Dolgain when the soldiers took possession of the valley. The scar left by the lightning remained on his neck. They were a family of good tenors, and of course the grandfather of Mrs D.M. Davies, Glantegid was William Eden Williams, the poet from Dolmynach, where the unfortunate family stayed for six months in the old house. I heard my father say that there had been three huge lightning bolts, and there was an unusually harsh winter afterwards.

Regarding burials at Penstryd cemetery, anecdotal evidence suggests that an entire generation were not buried there, because families did not wish for their loved ones to lie there in the sound of constant artillery fire and they were therefore interred at Pencefn, Trawsfynydd's village graveyard.

The gravestone of Morris and Robert Jones, David and Gwen Jones' children. Gwen's grave is immediately to the right

Over:
Moon over the Feidiogydd

Before The Soldiers Arrived

The names of the farms and smallholdings in Cwm Dolgain before the arrival of the army were:

Buarth Brwynog: upper eastern end of the valley

Hafod Garreg: near Buarth Brwynog

Nant Lliwgys: between Pont Cain and Buarth Brwynog

Hafoty Llelo (Hafoty'r Plas): between Craiglaseithin and Afon Cain

Gelli Gain: the lower side of the Llanuwchllyn road beneath Pig Idris

Llech Idris: slightly north of the Menhir of the same name

Dolmoch: on Ffridd Dol Moch – Dolmoch Isaf and Dolmoch Uchaf can be found about 200 metres from each other

Dolmynach: Not far north of Pont Dolmynach on the eastern side of Afon Cain

Dolmynach Isaf: near Pont y Llyn Du

Feidiog (Defeidiog) Uchaf: on the Feidiog moorland

Feidiog Bach (Defeidiog Ganol): on the Feidiog moorland

Feidiog (Defeidiog) Isaf (Danger Farm): on Ffridd Harri Howel mountain pasture near the confluence of Nant Ganol and Nant Hir

Tŷ Clap: on Llech Idris land

Foty Bryn Prys (unknown)

Foty Harri Howel (unknown)

Cae Gwragedd: on Dolgain land

Maesclawddffridd: on Hafoty Bach land, opposite Dolgain

Hafoty Bach: on the eastern side of Beddcoedwr road

Penmaen: south of Graig Penmaen

Tyddyn Gwladys: south of Bont Rhyd y Dail (Pont Gwynfynydd)

Penygraig: in the Craig Penmaen area

Part 2

Here we will have a more detailed look at the firing range – the need for it in the first place, what type of exercise was taking place there and the need to extend the range and the protests that were made against that.

Introduction

The history of the establishment of the Ranges at Cwm Dolgain, near Bronaber, dates back to the early twentieth century. Previously it was a peaceful valley with the land carefully cultivated by generations of farmers associated with the smallholdings and farms that existed there. However, in terms of the bigger picture, up to this period Britain considered itself essentially as a maritime force, retaining only a small professional army to protect its interests overseas. But, as a result of weaknesses discovered during the Boer Wars, South Africa (1899-1902), together with concern about the motivation of the German, Russian and Austrian rulers and emperors, regarding their tendency towards expansion of their lands and indeed their personal hatred towards each other, Hungary persuaded Lord Haldane, the Secretary of State for War, that the British military structure needed to be re-examined.

Thus, to preserve the strength of the standing army, Haldane decided to establish a second line out of a mixture of militia, volunteers and yeomen that had been created to defend Britain at the time of the Napoleonic wars. This was the Territorial Force (later the Territorial Army) and they were equipped and structured as the standing army in units that would reinforce the standing army in foreign countries. This resulted in the Territorial Army having to receive field training in artillery firing jointly with the Royal Artillery. Hence artillery exercises therefore started in the Cwm Dolgain in 1903.

First day of firing, 1903

Danger Farm

Following a visit from a War Office official in the company of Mr O. Yale and Mr John Lloyd Jones of Blaenau Ffestiniog in April 1900, it was considered that the area was suitably favourable for the encampment of artillery forces. As a result, the first seasonal military camp was seen on the Bryngolau farm fields in 1903 to 1904, and a familiar view for Hedd Wyn and his family was to see soldiers marching through the Ysgwrn farmyard before climbing over Ffridd Ddu into Cwm Dolgain to practice. The first year of practice saw the arrival of 14 regiments of the Royal Field Artillery as well as 3 regiments of the Royal Horse Artillery. These included 3,000 men, 1,500 horses and 102 howitzers.

Bryngolau Camp, near Yr Ysgwrn

After this in 1905, the army purchased Rhiwgoch and the lands of Cwm Dolgain for practice and camping purposes. The exercises would take place in the initial years between early March and the end of September. There was a considerable increase in exercises during the period of the Great War, with the place also being used as a German prisoner of war camp. As commercialism increased, a small purpose-built village was established, named after a nearby farm of Bronaber and was soon referred to as 'Tin-town'.

By the Second World War, the tents had been replaced by more permanent structures as accommodation. The site was again used as a prisoner of war camp although, this time, Italians rather than Germans were the prisoners.

After World War II, the camp became less important, but it was used as an explosives demolition area for unused weapons, these were transported by rail to Trawsfynydd, and then on trucks to Mynydd Bach in order to blow them up.

1. Horse stuck in the peat; 2. Bryngolau Camp, 1903; 3. Man-handling a big gun on first day of firing 26.06.1903; 4. Troops mustering; 5. Every man and his dog viewing the first day of firing 26.06.1903

The Land – From South Africa to Cwm Dolgain

The Boer wars had a great deal of influence over the decision to use Cwm Dolgain for a number of reasons. Firstly, British military wars had taken place on Europe's relatively flat continent, where the enemy were able to see each other within the length of a few fields. In South Africa the land was more mountainous and, as a result, a new technique of firing at an unseen enemy, who was safely behind the natural defence of the country's landscape, had to be used to all intents and purposes. To this end, Cwm Dolgain was found to be very similar to the South African lands because of its mountainous location. Indeed, following the first exercises in 1903, many soldiers who had seen action on the battlefields of South Africa, mentioned how similar the landscape was to that of Transvaal and the then Orange River Colony. The valley's peatland was also ideal as it would allow the shells to sink into it without causing damage and shrapnel to the same extent that would be on more solid terrain. This of course caused long-term problems for the MoD as the shells regularly worked themselves to the surface and as a result had to be collected and made safe until relatively recently.

The army originally bought 6,177 acres for the purpose of artillery firing, including the lands of Cwm Dolgain and Rhiwgoch east of the A470 with pieces of land near Glan Llynnau Duon and Crawcwellt to the west – where the big guns would fire over the Camp and Penstryd Chapel as far as the mountain pastures of Harri Howel, Bryn Pierce and Dol Moch.

Bearing in mind South Africa's connection, it is interesting to note that when looking at a map of the firing range made in 1911, the surveyor referred to one of the folds on the Dol Moch mountain pasture as 'Kraal', a South African word for a sheepfold.

The map also shows that the army had built a new road from the crossroads of Rhiwgoch to Penstryd. Originally the road would go straight up steeply over the hill from the crossroads, something that was

1. Big Guns Firing;
2. Trawsfynydd Firing Ranges;
3. "Tin Town" Bronaber hamlet

not ideal for horse-drawn gun carriages, so a northerly route was taken following around the hill's contour and gradually rising to Penstryd, the road was called 'North Stafford Road' – and this is still in daily use to go to Cwm Dolgain.

Another interesting feature of the above map is the reference to 'Bathing Pool' in one of the oxbow lakes of the River Eden between Orsedd Las and Ynys Thomas. A welcome amenity no doubt for soldiers to go bathing on a nice summer evening!

The land belonged to the estate of Sir Watkin Williams-Wynn of Wynnstay and was purchased by the War Department on the 20th March 1905 for £28,500. The table below, which has been reproduced from the original deeds, notes the different sites and their size:

North Camp from North Stafford Road

No. on rental	Tenement		Acreage		
			A.	R.	P.
1673	Hendre Caerhonydd (part of) *		40	1	19
1674a	Dolymoch		201	3	31
1674	Tyddyndu		178	1	16
1675	Defeidiog Ganol		128	2	7
1676	Defeidiog-isaf		394	2	2
1678	Dolymynach		204	1	31
1679	Dolhaidd		118	3	10
1679a	Part of Dolydd Prysor and Buarth Brwynog		171	0	13
1681	Glanllyniau		53	2	6
1682	Gilfachwen		177	1	6
1683	Gors		238	0	8
1683a	Gelligain		87	2	23
1684	Llech Idris	128a. 1p. 35p.			
1685 pt.	Hafod y Garreg	69a. 0r. 24p.	197	2	19
1686	Rhiwgoch and Penstryd		501	3	18
1686a	Tynllain (originally part of Rhiwgoch and Gilfachwen)		6	1	16
1688	Tyddynmawr		289	1	26

Unenclosed land

1685 pt.	Deugain		36	0	11
	Mynydd Bach	about 523a. 0r. 24p.			
	Mynydd Dolymoch	about 1050a. 0r. 31p.	1573	1	15
	Mynydd Penstryd		1577	0	1
			6177	0	38

* *Hendre Caerhonydd = Hendre Bryncrogwydd?*

Over:
Danger Explosives Sign

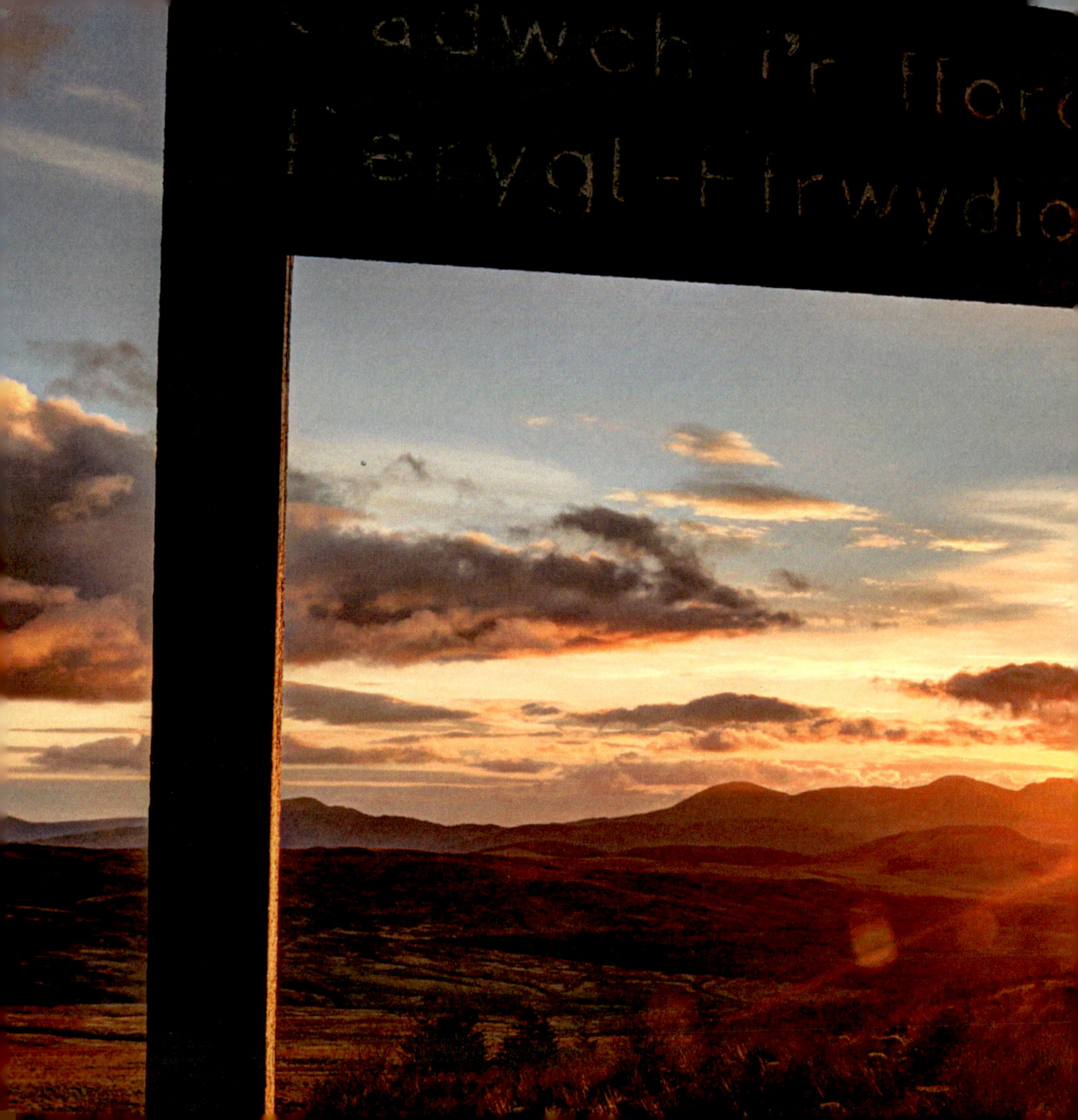

Transport Problems

Trawsfynydd railway station was the soldiers' first introduction to the area before proceeding on their way to Bronaber. In the early years this meant that the men and their horses, which were drawing the big guns, had to pass through the village and this was not an easy feat either. Firstly, the steep hill of Rhiw Pen Cefn from the Station had to be negotiated down towards the centre of the village. There was a risk of horses losing control of their heavy load, which would happen from time to time and, as a result, two escape refuges were built into the massive retaining walls so that a pedestrian could escape into them should such an emergency occur.

The second problem was ascending the hill towards Highgate (now called Llys Ednowain) and turning tightly at the junction near Glasfryn – the road was steeper and narrower at that time. In order to solve the problem, the Royal Engineers proposed building a new road along a section of the old Roman road, Sarn Helen; over to Wern Gron then turning west and link back to the village near Trawsfynydd Bridge. This proposal had been the subject of discussion by the Parish Council for almost two years up to December 1906. It is not clear what was impeding their decision, especially since highways were clearly the responsibility of the County Council, a point they made to the War Office more than once. In any event, the army agreed to contribute £1,000 towards the road provided that the County Council then took responsibility for it in respect of its maintenance – so the Parish Council agreed to support the scheme.

Military Station

While things were more convenient now to move weapons, men and horses to Bronaber, it was creating congestion at the railway station, which now had to deal with civilian use, goods and troops with all their equipment. Thus in 1911 a special military station was built to the north of the original one, Stesion Newydd ('New Station') as it was known colloquially. The new station cost £10,030 and consisted of

1. Map from 1911 showing extent of firing range; 2. Returning from practice; 3. Preparing for exercise

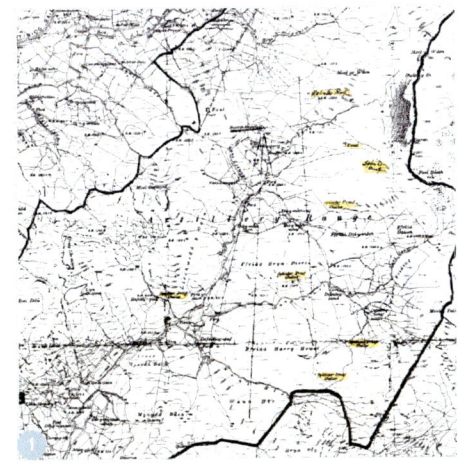

two platforms, one at 477 feet in length and the other at 451 feet. A wooden screen was built 7 feet tall along the platform so that it screened the main line movements from the horses' sight (but not the sound!). Included in the military yard were buildings such as a warehouse, two toilet blocks and a guard room.

Looking at an example of a notice of 'Special Troop Trains from Trawsfynydd to Reading and Swindon Town on June 19th 1919', it is interesting to note the following:

Danger Farm

	Officers	Men	Guns and Limbers	Chargers	Horses	4-Wheel Wagons	2-Wheel Wagons	Cycles	Baggage Tons
No. 3	-	-	-	-	215	-	-	-	-
No. 4	4	77	4	6	164	1	2	-	4

No. 3 Train for Reading
No. 4 Train for Swindon Town

It's amazing for us today to appreciate how many horses were used by the soldiers, as seen from the table above there was a total of 385 of them (including the 'Chargers').

It was not only horses that were seen there, but also mules, as David Moelwyn Evans, the son of the village policeman remembered in a newspaper article he wrote once. "It was an unforgettable time for us as children to visit the Military Station to see the soldiers arriving in in their thousands mostly on Sundays. It was great fun to watch the old mules with guns on their backs and often refusing to move an inch. I remember one soldier asking me to "hold the head" of one of these creatures, but the old mule took one respectable look at me and pinched me in my hand. I let go of him immediately, and the last time I saw him, he was galloping in the direction of Cwm Prysor and as far as I know, he's still there!"

On the 29th of August 1907, there was an accident with a train that was in use by the 53rd Battery, Royal Field Artillery. This happened whilst shunting with the train split in two. Unfortunately, the brake had not been applied on the first part, so when the loco tried to buffer with it, it was driven forward with considerable force to the second part causing extensive damage. Two drivers and two soldiers were injured in the incident.

Quite large trains were seen with double header locomotives (two engines connected together) that were used to pull due to the length and weight of the train. As there was a relatively steep gradient upwards from Bala to Cwm Prysor Halt, sometimes banking support would be required from another loco, that is,

1. *Grenade Range at Bryn Perfedd;*
2. *Mills grenade*

pushing the train from behind. To avoid disrupting the railway's daily schedule, the military trains would run mostly on Sundays.

It's worth noting that in the early years the troops, horses and guncarriages, would sometimes return to their respective bases via Dolgellau railway station.

There were special stables for the horses in the camp and they would take them for exercise walks on Sundays from Bronaber to where the former Nuclear Power Stations entrance is now, before returning back for the camp. You can just imagine the extraordinary noise made by about a hundred horses with the clatter of their hooves on the road through the village. Following objections from Chapel Ministers, Mr Evan Jones, clerk to the Parish Council, wrote to complain to the War Office about Sunday movements in June 1910, with the Director of the War Office responding by asking him for examples with the dates and names of the units.

Some years later in February 1914, a petition was signed by about 600 local inhabitants once again complaining about the inconvenience to religious services caused by troop movements on Sundays.

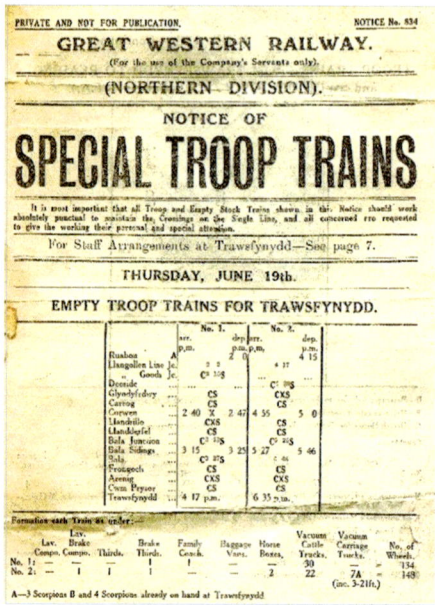

Special Troop Train Notice

1. Military Station today;
2. The Military Station;
3. Trouble loading a horse

Danger Farm

Indian Army

Transportation was a problem later in the Second World War as well when 'K Force' from the RIASC ('Royal Indian Army Service Corp') established themselves for a few months in the area. The reason behind this was that the British Army was now almost totally mechanical regarding transport, but wet weather in Europe created great difficulties for them with the vehicles and lorries getting stuck in the mud! As a result, it was not possible to advance forward or make any other progress, and the only friendly army in the world still using mules was the Indian Army. So, at the request of the British government, Indian troops and their mules volunteered to assist, and the war effort was soon back on its feet. 'K Force' was an unarmed company in Dunkirk and as a result of their experiences it was decided that they should receive training in weapons use and so they came to practice to Traws in the spring months of 1942. Their meat-eating traditions and their different faith meant that they were allowed to keep their sheep in a field in the Station area in order to kill them in the 'Halal' style. To this end, it is seen from Trawsfynydd '47 Supply Depot' diaries, on the 28th March 1942, for that purpose, that, 'Six butchers despatched by rail to Trawsfynnedd' (sic).

RIASC Soldiers on Parade

Over:
Rainbow over the Ranges

Social

Like in every age, the soldiers liked going for a couple of pints and there's a humorous little anecdote about them at the Ring (Cross Foxes). Miss Pugh of Bryn Gwyn, a well-to-do landowner, had sold a plot of land to the community to create a memorial garden in memory of those who lost their lives in the Great War, namely Bryn y Gofeb. She also allowed her gardener to oversee and maintain the site. In any case, it had been a very wet summer, almost impossible to grow any flowers or vegetables and both were discussing this problem.

Miss Pugh asked how the gardening was coming along and the gardener answered, 'I'm afraid Miss Pugh that this constant rain makes it impossible to cultivate the land or the flowers.' She said, 'O dear, shame about that.' The gardener went on to ask, 'Miss Pugh, do you know what *glaw* (rain) is in English?' She certainly knew, but probably in order to be sociable she pretended not to know. 'Well, Miss Pugh I've been listening to the soldiers in the Ring and I've heard them say several times that it's "F... ing rain".'

The gardener of course said this in pure innocence as Welsh was his only language – goodness knows what Miss Pugh thought!

Equally, some locals would visit the Camp for a drink on a Sunday, since the village pubs were shut on the day of the Lord, with a few being fined for being "drunk and disorderly on the Sabbath" – a serious offence in the early part of the 20th century!

When the military camp was at its busiest in the early decades of the last century, the soldiers would come with their soiled clothes to be washed by the housewives of Stryd Faen (Stone Street), and one of those would be responsible for carrying gallons of water from the nearby well of Ffynnon Cwrclis for the purpose of the weekly laundry. The few pennies the housewives gained were a very welcome addition to their housekeeping allowance. Whilst they were there with their clothes, the soldiers would leave their horses to graze at Cae Garnau field, behind Stryd Faen. They would then take the opportunity to buy a bottle of 'Elin Owen's Beer' from over the rear wall of the adjoining Smithy, at thru pence a bottle!

There are also examples of some farms in the area benefiting from the soldiers' food waste for the purpose of pig feed free of charge.

Anti-social

Unfortunately, there are a few examples of soldiers behaving in an unacceptable manner, thieving in particular. Below are a couple of examples that found their way into the newspapers of the day.

In July 1903, four soldiers were accused of stealing 23 shillings from Defeidiog Ganol farmhouse between the hours of 9:00am and 4:00pm. They were H. Sarfas, J. Baines, W. Clowes and J. McIntyre.

A constable informed the court that the artillery were firing in Cwm Dolgain and that between the hours of 9 and 4 the farmhouse families had to leave their houses and proceed to a sheltered location designated to them, prior to returning home once the firing had ceased. A pound had gone from a purse and about three shillings from a child's piggy bank during

Bryn y Gofeb, Remembrance Sunday 2014

the above hours and that this was proof enough that only the accused could have been there.

Hugh Rowlands and Edward Rowlands from Defeidiog Ganol, stated that their farm was within the firing area and that they had barred the rear door and locked the front one at eight in the morning. However, when they returned at about five, they became suspicious upon seeing the back-door bar loose and both purse and piggy bank emptied.

Sergeant W. George Faro confirmed that he was supervising the firing area on

Penstryd Gun Park

Danger Farm

the day. At about nine o clock he went to the splinter shelter which was about 800 yards from the farmhouse. On his way there he saw Sarfas and Clowes taking two horses towards the farm to be watered. He ordered them not to go near nor enter the house, but if it started to rain, they could shelter in the yard out-house. He later saw Baines and McIntyre go to the same place with their horses. He was in constant view of the place and was quite certain that only those four were there between the aforementioned times. It was discovered that McIntyre had 6s 7½d and Baines had 5s 2½d on them.

PC Griffith testified that Sarfas and Baines admitted to being in the house and eating bread and butter and had some milk to drink, but they knew nothing about the money. The four said they were not guilty of the charges against them. Each then gave their own defence stating that they were in the house and helped themselves to milk, bread and butter.

Lieutenant Thornburn Mc Gower stated that Sarfas was of particularly good character. Clowes had only been known to him for a year. The officer made no reference to the other two.

The bench retired and subsequently released Sarfas. It was noted that farmers' properties needed to be safeguarded under such extreme circumstances in the firing area and ordered the other three to be jailed for a month with hard labour.

Then in May 1909, Eli Chubb a soldier from the Camp was accused of breaking into Maengwyn in the village. The residents, Thomas Evans, and his sister Jane Evans, upon their return to the house discovered that a break-in had occurred, with the back door open and a broken window with blood on the glass. Whilst they inspected the property, they heard a noise in the back and someone running away. Chubb apologized for his actions and said that it was because he had been drinking. He had been in the army for 4 years and said his wages were only twelve shillings a week. The charge of house breaking was reduced to that of being somewhere without legal permission to be there. He was subsequently fined ten shillings and a further ten shillings and ten pence in costs.

Poor wages, boredom and alcohol were certainly not good for morale, and perhaps that is why we find a note about deserters found at Dyffryn in the Cambrian News back in May 1906. "Two soldiers, who deserted from the artillery camp at Trawsfynydd, were on Monday arrested at Dyffryn by PC Davies and locked up till an escort arrived to convey them back to the camp."

Bye-laws

I previously referred to the uneasy relationship and the disputes that arose from time to time between the Parish Council of Traws and the military authorities, and this was useful because it gives us an insight into the socio-economic culture of the period, as we see in the saga of the 1908 Bye-laws.

The Parish Council wrote to the War Office on the 11th of February 1908 to state their opposition to the content of a draft of the Bye-laws and as a result the Camp Brigadier held a meeting with the Council in order to appease them and to propose a compromise.

Three major issues appear to require attention by the Council and need to be included as such in the Bye-laws, namely, what to do when it is necessary to cross the Firing Range in an emergency, fair day firing routines and the procedure in relation to sheep that had been killed. To this effect the 'Special Instructions Relating to the Bye-Laws for the Trawsfynydd Artillery Range' was provided. A note at the top of this annex to the Bye-laws indicates that these only referred to the year 1908.

On the matter of crossing the ranges in an emergency from the direction of Bryn Gath to the Dol Mynach Bridge; a flagpole would be installed on the eastern boundary of the War Office lands with a yellow flag on it to be raised in an emergency. Another yellow flag would be raised to acknowledge the request by the troops on their lands of Ffridd Cefn Llwyd. The person would then have to pull the flag down and hastily cross to Penstryd. It was noted that this should only be done in the event of a major emergency!

There is a humorous anecdotal account of a person from the Abergeirw area who ventured in the direction of Traws without going through the procedure of raising the yellow flag. He went on across the Range, and after he

1. *Penstryd Sentry Box; 2. Fence posts from former fence to reduce sheep casualties; 3. Moel Oernant flag foundation; 4. Old shells on top of Ffridd Wen boundary wall*

reached the sentry box at Penstryd he was stopped by the sergeant on duty and received a firm reprimand from him for his folly. He then shared his experience with a friend who asked him what the sergeant had said to him. 'I didn't quite understand him properly,' he said, 'but he shouted something about blow your f...ing head off!' It should be remembered in this context that English was an alien language to the area at that time, although, I think the message was quite clear!

The parish fairs were the second issue of concern. There were four fairs held in the parish, important seasonal job fairs in order to assist with farm labour needs. So, on a fair day, it was agreed that no firing would start before 10:00 o'clock in the morning and finish as soon as possible thereafter and there would be no firing at night on fair days. Also, the Parish Council would have to give good notice of the dates of the fairs to the Army.

Sheep
The third major issue was sheep, or rather what to do with those who had been accidentally killed. Rule 7 said that sheep killed would be left untouched for 24 hours, but no longer. In Rule 8 it was noted that recognition of the claim for killed sheep would be provided by the relevant officer.

By 1941 more comprehensive Bye-laws were issued which clarified the rights of the Army to fire with any weapon of any kind when the red flags were flown and clarification of the boundaries of the area as well as the location of the red flags which were as follows:

1. FFRIDD CEFN LLWYD
2. CRAIG-LAS-EITHIN
3. MOEL OERNANT
4. GALLT-Y-DARREN
5. PEN-Y-FEIDIOG
6. PEN-Y-CWM
7. PANT GLAS Gate.

It was an offence for anyone without consent to be in the danger area, including any vehicle, animal or thing, other than grazing animals at the owner's risk. A fine of up to £5 would be given to any offender with the additional right to seize and forfeit any vehicle, animal or thing that would have been left in the area.

Special attention was paid to doctors and the like in connection with an emergency crossing from the direction of

Bryn Gath to Penstryd or the Pont Llyn Du bridge to Penstryd in rule 3(i). They would have to inform the sentry on duty and then wait until he had received the Commanding Officer's permission for them to pass. For any others, they would have to introduce themselves to the sentry at midday at the gate of Pant Glas, Penstryd or Pont Llyn Du and if circumstances allowed, they could then cross.

The 'Special Precautions' towards the back of the document again address sheep by referring to a fence that was 2,500 yards long at the eastern side of Llechwedd y Gain and west of the river Cain for the purpose of reducing injuries to sheep. Incidentally, some of the old fence posts are still standing to this day. It was said that a sheep killed by a shell was worth more than one in the mart – as a result, and strangely, gaps appeared in the fence quite often! The ears of the sheep were then to be taken to the duty officer at 'Danger Farm' (the former Feidiog Isa' farmhouse) in order to receive compensation for it.

The shells were not the only problem for them either. The late Hugh Rowlands, Dolgain, whilst shepherding the area discovered a number of them at periods of winter weather buried under heavy snow in the 'dug outs' and had consequently died.

The Trawsfynydd Tragedy

Whilst the Bye-laws were quite explicit about the dangers of entering the range and indeed bilingual warning signs were placed in several areas to further emphasise the lethal nature of the weapons and not to touch any such unexploded munitions if found, sadly this advice was not always apparent, as can be seen from a report in the Cambrian News in October 1908.

Robert Roberts was only 15years old and employed at Tanrallt Farm, Cwm Prysor, he was killed by tampering with a live shell. He was the son of Mr William Roberts, Mill Cottage, Llandderfel. It appeared that he had picked it up from the hills adjoining the artillery range on a Sunday. He took it to the farmhouse and placed it behind the kitchen door. When the farmer, John Roberts, saw it he threw it into the yard where it remained until the following day when the lad was seen with a hammer striking it with the intention of trying to open it. The shell immediately burst and blew him to pieces with portions of his body blown to the adjoining stream. Dr Humphreys who attended the scene, said the shell when it burst apparently caught the lad in the chest. John Roberts, who also received severe shrapnel wounds to his arm from the blast, said that he had warned the lad not to touch the shell.

Captain Coningham, H.M. Inspector of explosives, emphasised the danger of tampering with live shells – it was believed that the shell was probably a 50 or 60 pounder. He explained that unexploded shells were in a more sensitive condition than ordinary shells and would often burst on the least touch. Many accidents had happened in this way. They should be left alone and reported to the police or military authorities.

A verdict of Accidental Death was passed at the inquest as well as a resolution to ask the War Office to issue warning notices annually to neighbouring farmers and that they should be in Welsh. It was pointed out that annual notices were important due to occasional changes of tenancy.

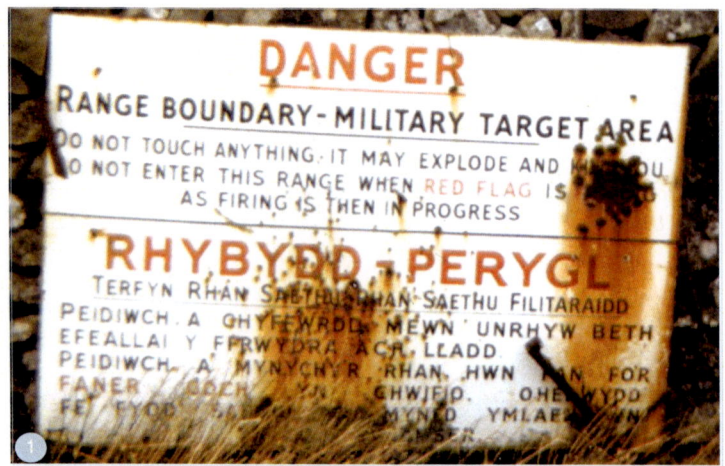

1. Bilingual range danger sign. Range boundary – military target area. Do not touch anything, it may explode and kill you. Do not enter this range when red flag is flying as firing is then in progress; 2. Tanrallt Farm, Cwm Prysor; 3. A spent shell laying on the Range

Balloon

As I mentioned before, fighting on mountainous terrain, such as South Africa in the Boer Wars, had shown that a new technique of artillery firing was necessary without seeing the enemy. One of the techniques used was the observation balloon.

Such a balloon was located at the Camp and was kept in a special station known to this day as *Twll Balŵn* (balloon hole). The site is seen on the right-hand side of the road leading from Rhiwgoch to Gilfachwen – there are also the remains of four iron rings there used to anchor the balloon. A balloon from a Frenchman's design, Caquot, was used at the Camp, with three fins in order to stabilize it in the air. It was hydrogen gas that allowed it to fly with two observers on board, or rather in a wickerwork basket hanging from the underside. They had binoculars, radio and long-range cameras in order to keep track of the exercises and to give instructions regarding the location of the targets.

With that background, there's an interesting article that appeared in *The Times* on the 13th June 1930 – which carried the striking headline: 'Adrift In Balloon – Flying Officer Suspended Head Downwards'. The article describes how Flying Officer Pelham Groom and Sergeant G.W. Robinson had an 'exciting adventure' after their balloon broke free from its anchorage and drifted 15 miles away! Both were members of the Royal Air Force (RAF) 'Kite Balloon Detachment' which was located at the Camp. They had been observing the firing exercise when it broke loose as it was pulled down (some think it wasn't by accident!). They found that they quickly ascended to a height of a few thousand feet. It then drifted over the Arenig mountains towards Bala. The report also says that at one time they almost hit electric wires! In the Cwm Tirmynach area, the balloon came down close enough to the ground for both to try to jump out. Robinson had succeeded but injured his eye and found himself disorientated for a moment. When he

1. *"Twll Balŵn" (Balloon hole) Balloon Station; 2. Observation Balloon above the Camp; 3. Balloon anchor ring*

stood up, he noticed that the balloon was drifting again and that Pelham Groom, in trying to jump out, had unfortunately got one leg stuck in the basket and as a result he was hanging head down from the device! Robinson followed the balloon as it struck against the ground every now and again before ascending once more with the officer desperately trying to get his leg loose. The report goes on to say that Robinson had run two miles over hedges, shrubs, bogs and ditches before catching up with the balloon at Hafod yr Esgob farm and then releasing Pelham Groom, who despite the escapade was uninjured. The balloon continued on its journey towards Corwen's direction. 'I owe my life to the brave action of Sergeant Robinson' said Flying Officer Pelham Groom after the incident.

Buffalo Bill's Son

While the wind was the great enemy of the balloon, it was the good friend of the kite – and that's where Buffalo Bill's son comes into the story, or S.F. Cody to use his proper name. The agent of William Cody (the original Buffalo Bill) took legal action against S.F. Cody to prevent him from calling himself 'Son of Buffalo Bill'. Both had a Wild West Show and they looked pretty similar to each other and that was probably the cause of the contention (with S.F. taking advantage of the other one's name).

Cody camped under canvas at the Camp from the 6th to 17th August, 1906. The reason behind this was that Cody had devised a kite that could carry a man for

Alan Ladd on location at the Ranges during filming the Red Beret in 1952

observation purposes. Cody was mostly recognized as an entertainer; however, he was also a successful businessman and inventor. As a result, the British Army signed an agreement with him to be responsible for the design and production of a kite as well as the chief trainer for kites. The wording of his commission, which was for a period of two years, said, 'Mr Cody's status is the same as that of an officer in His Majesty's Army, although he has no military authority'.

So, we see that the purpose of Buffalo Bill's son stay at the Camp was to train soldiers on how to fly a kite.

Alan Ladd
Another American who visited the Camp and filmed on a location on Mynydd Bach in the Ranges in 1953 was Alan Ladd, the actor from Hollywood. He was here to film *The Red Beret* with a number of other stars of the period including Stanley Baker, the Welshman from Ferndale, Glamorgan. This was a fictional film about an American pretending to be a Canadian in order to join the British Parachute Regiment in the Second World War. Regarding the film's accuracy, according to the web site ParaData, which is responsible

S.F. Cody's two-man kite

for recording the history of the Regiment; it would be better for any military historian researching authentic technical achievements by the regiment in the Second World War, to search elsewhere!

Improperly Dressed
John "O'B" O'Brien, the author's father, started his working life in the famous

Docks of the city of Liverpool. He joined the Army in Colchester at the age of eighteen to do his national service with the Royal Army Ordnance Corps and specifically No 1 EDU (Explosives Demolition Unit). He had pneumonia while in Colchester and was sent home. After his health improved, he went back there, but his troop had gone to Germany by then. So after about a year in the Army he was sent to Traws.

1. The Camp's former cinema; 2. The Camp's Post Office; 3. The Camp's Canteen; 4. Officers' tents near Rhiwgoch

Danger Farm

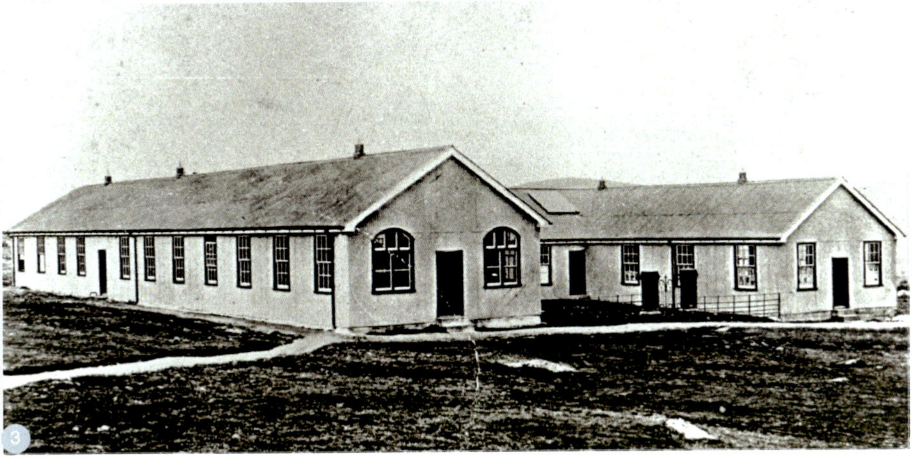

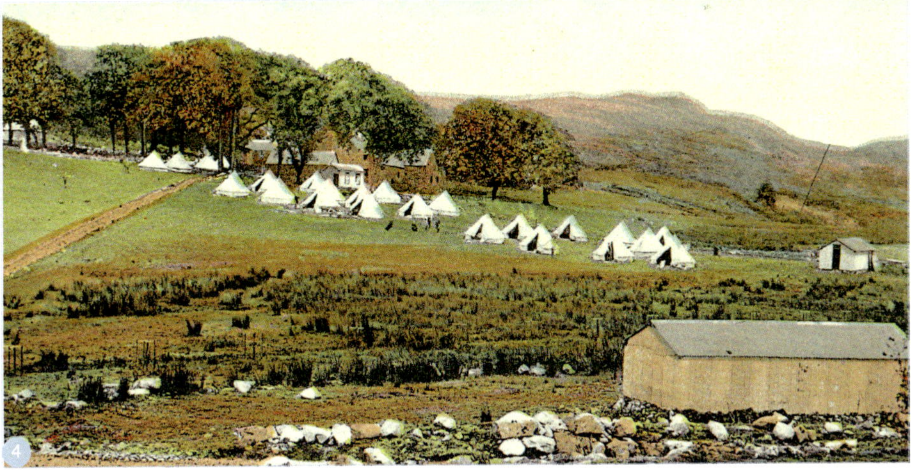

1. Big gun with tractor; 2. Horse-drawn ambulance – note the red cross on the canvas covering; 3. North Camp and gun park; 4. South Camp and gun park

One day while O'B and his friend were leaving the Cross Foxes in their military uniforms they were reported for being "improperly dressed" by an Army officer from South Wales who happened to be in the village at the time. This was due to them having their tunic buttons undone and their berets tucked under their shoulder epaulettes. As punishment, he and his friend were sent to Cairnryan near Stranraer where they assisted in loading toxic gas canisters on board a ship for disposal at sea. The weather was too inclement to do this one day, so he and his friend were given orders to clean the Sergeant's Mess. However, they were soon arrested and placed behind bars and were accused of stealing money from the Mess till. But it soon transpired that the

Sergeant that had placed them on cleaning duty was the person that had stolen the money! O'B was called in front of the CO who sincerely apologised to him and asked what he could do to make things right. "I want to go back to Traws, Sir", said O'B, with his mate adding "I want to go with him". And so it was, he returned to the camp at Bronaber and was met by his old Colour Sergeant Major at the entrance to the camp who greeted him with, "Oh no, not you again!!!"

The main duty he had while in the camp was to blow up unused second world war munitions on Mynydd Bach at 4.00 pm every day.

As mentioned, No 1 EDU had an active role in the Camp and a story that he would recount from time to time was about the sheep that were marked ED, denoting the initials of the farmer that owned them. Mysteriously on occasion an additional "U" could be seen on some of the sheep, the mark then being EDU!

1. O'B relaxing off-duty back at Traws, following his unpleasant experience at Cairnryan; 2. Mynydd Bach (middle) from Llechweddgain observatory; 3. Scammel Pioneer 6x4 stuck at Mynydd Bach

Over: Military telegraph pole

More Land Needed

In this part of the history we will have the opportunity to look back at the inquiry that took place in relation to the Army's need to get more land to practice.

There was already 8,403 acres belonging to the Army, most of Cwm Dolgain with another piece of land to practice grenade throwing between the river Eden and the A470 just south of Bronaber. They now wanted an additional 5,120 acres for technical reasons, namely that the latest shells could reach further, and in terms of safety in relation to the wider area of the shellburst in the danger area. There was also a need for more land due to the increase in numbers of the National Standing Army Service and National Territorial Army Service soldiers.

'Butter not Guns'

The War Office's request was subject to an inquiry by the Town and Country Planning Ministry, presided over by Sir Wyn Wheldon. The inquiry was located at Dolgellau Magistrates Court and it commenced on 18th November, 1949.

There were a large number of students protesting from Welsh universities who were seen outside the court marching in front of the building and carrying placards with the slogans, 'Butter Not Guns' and 'Not an Inch of Welsh Land' on them. There was a significant audience there to hear the case with seventeen different organisations taking part.

Barrister Jones-Roberts and the clerk Hugh J. Owen represented Merioneth County Council, Deudraeth and Penllyn Rural Councils, Trawsfynydd, Llanuwchllyn and Llanycil Parish Councils. On behalf of Meirionnydd NFU and the Meirionnydd Land Protection Committee, V. Lloyd-Jones K.C. and D. Watkin Powell appeared.

On the opposing side the War Office was represented by Major-General G.N. Wood, Brigadier G.H.P. Whitfield, Lieutenant-Colonel T.H.F. Foulkes, Brigadier W.R. Goodman and C.H.W. Murphy.

1. Protesting outside Dolgellau Court with Major-General Wood talking to the protesters; 2. Map showing the additional land required by the army

YMENYN
NID
CYNNAU
DIM

To FESTINIOG
0 Miles 2 4
N
BALA
TRAWSFYNYDD
Lake BALA
To DOLGELLEY
LLANUWCHLLYN
EXISTING RANGE (8.403acres)
PROPOSED EXTENSION (5.120acres)
FIRING AREA
BATTLE AREA
To DOLGELLEY
NON FIRING AREA
ASSEMBLY AREA

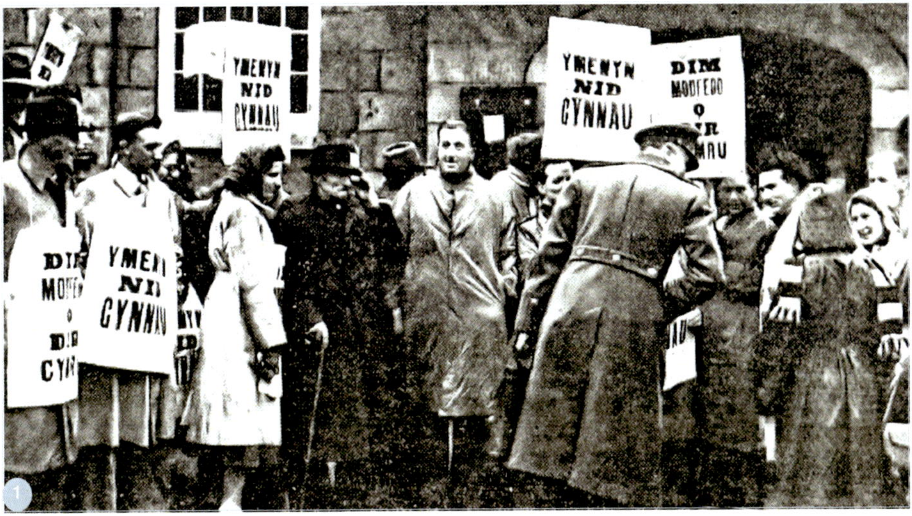

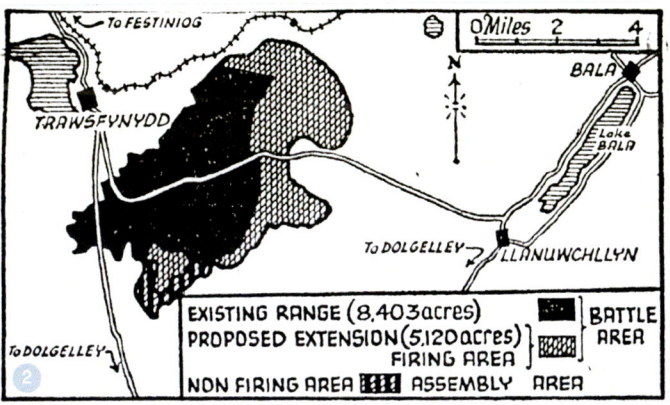

Major-General Wood stated that he was responsible for the 53rd Welsh Division and in peaceful times his duty was to train the division. He added that he had been in the two Great Wars and one of the saddest things to see was the loss of young lives due to a lack of adequate training.

Land Sacrifice

He went on to say that Dorset, his home county, shared the same land sacrifices and amenities as Meirionnydd for military training. They asked for 13,420 of Meirionnydd's acres to enable the army to exercise in places called practical training areas and Trawsfynydd would be the location of the Western Command area. Such an area would allow a soldier to use his weapons by firing live munitions under the tactical circumstances of modern battlefields. The arms here would range from rifles to big guns. He suggested that refusing to allow a soldier an opportunity to practise in this manner would be as irrational as refusing a sailor to use the sea or a pilot to use the air.

He added that the so-called 'push-button' war and the atomic bomb had not diminished the need for well-trained soldiers who were confident with their arms and prepared to fight with the enemy.

He went on to explain why Trawsfynydd had been chosen and said that the first and most obvious reason was that they already had 8,020 acres in their ownership and that they had been practicing artillery fire, firing mortars, machine guns and small arms there since 1908. He further explained that the land was of no agricultural value, nor a tourist attraction compared to the surrounding mountainous areas. On the other hand, the rough undulating terrain was well suited to military exercises.

It was noted that artillery exercise in the field was dependent not only on length but also in width and that an earlier plan had been omitted following discussions. Major-General Wood stated that the troops needed a southern assembly area near Dolgain Bridge for the soldiers to prepare for their attack on the appropriate combat area. No explosive warfare would be used in this area and it would be open to free use for agricultural purposes – subject to the nuisance of a few soldiers leaving gates open or some driver reversing into a gate-post, he could sympathise with this because he was a small-scale farmer himself.

'We don't want to damage amenity or agriculture,' he said. 'There will be no interference with agriculture and the mountain pastures will be retained. The tourist industry will not suffer because only a few tourists are seen to cross this isolated land.'

It was further explained that the army paid £452 a year in taxes in Meirionnydd and that their original employment list at the camp was 111, with a weekly wage bill of £554. It must be noted however that it is not clear if the numbers identified included the civilians employed to maintain the Camp and the roads etc., but what is important to realize is that a significant number of local people were also employed there.

One of those civilians was the late Richard Jones, Ty'n Llain, or Dick Ty'n Llain as everyone knew him. I remember Dick telling me a story about him as a lorry driver at the Camp and that he was ordered to go and collect a load of gravel to make concrete from the river Cain near Danger Farm. He had had to drive the wagon to the river to facilitate the loading, once the last bucket-full was poured, off he went. All was fine until Dick drove around a corner and saw a whole battalion marching along the road towards him and worse still a motorbike and sidecar was overtaking them, with an officer in the sidecar! He slammed his foot heavily on the brakes, but the truck did not slow down – because the brakes were wet after being in the river! With all the troops running out of harm's way he had no alternative but to steer the truck half-way up an embankment just as the motorbike and sidecar disappeared from sight. The truck overturned on its side with Dick curled up in a ball at the bottom of the cab, scared to come out as he thought he'd killed the motorbike rider and the officer. The next minute there was a soldier opening the passenger door, which was now facing the sky, shouting at him, 'Get out, the bloody wagon's on fire!' He was extremely grateful when he came out to discover that the driver and officer were uninjured – as the truck turned over they managed to get under it and escape unharmed!

Depopulation

Barrister Jones-Roberts stated that every inch of the land produced food and that experience showed wherever there was a military presence there was depopulation. He claimed that Trawsfynydd had depopulated twenty per cent in twenty years. Agriculture was the main industry with tourism a close second, adding that if there was a firing range, visitors would keep away from the area. He added that the area was at the centre of the proposed North Wales National Park and as a result a more repulsive proposition could not exist than that presented by the War Office. This was supported by D.R. Grenfell M.P., chair of the Wales Tourist and Holiday Board.

A large number of farmers also testified against the proposal and they were insistent that such intervention by the War Office would make it harder if not impossible to sustain a livelihood. They also claimed that the War Office did not pay fair compensation for sheep either, as they still paid out on the same rate set in 1908. In response to this, Captain G. Wilkinson said that this is correct as far as their tenants were concerned but wrong where there is a right to graze common land by others – in their case they received justifiable value for their sheep.

Another one who gave evidence was D.M. Ellis, a lecturer from Bangor Normal College. He said that an inexplicable special quality belonged to the area and one particular aspect of it was the Welshness of the area. If the English influence would be allowed to spread, it would be at the expense of everything dear to the Welsh. He said, 'We have given until we bleed,' then he added, 'There comes a time when such generosity cannot continue. Giving more in essence is harming us.'

The inquiry came to an end, however finding any information about its conclusion was long awaited, as the *Cambrian News* reported on the 14th July 1950:

The outcome of the Trawsfynydd land inquiry – such as news of the distribution of profits at the Dolgellau

1. *The Camp's civilian crew from the 1950's;*
2 *Camp workers circa 1986, many years after the army had left*

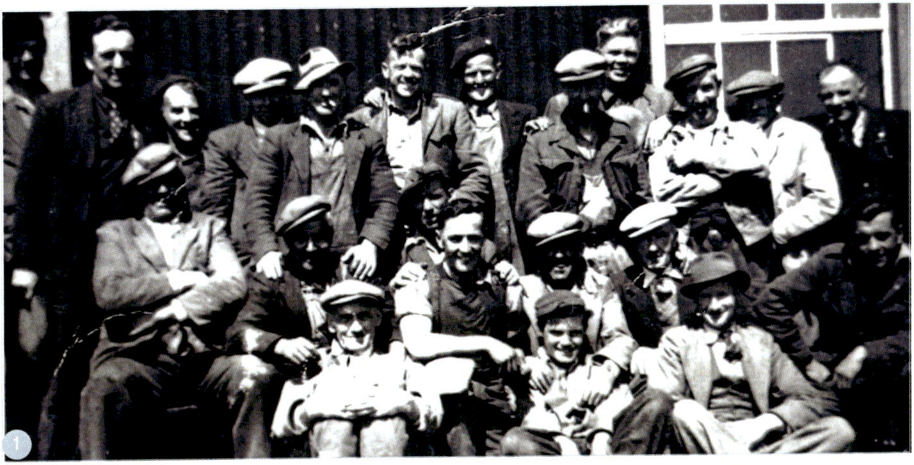
1

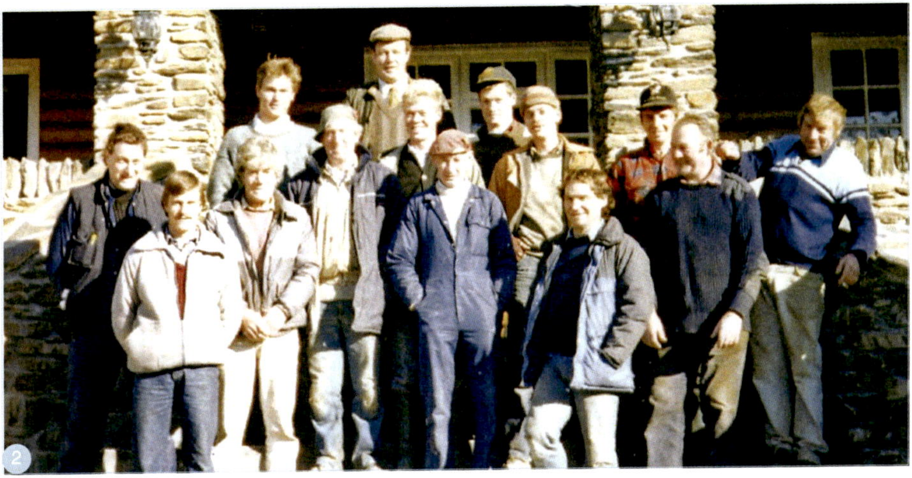
2

National Eisteddfod – is long overdue Sir Wyn Wheldon's inquiry last November created a great deal of commotion while it lasted. Since then not a word has been heard. Meanwhile military training is underway in Trawsfynydd, Llanbedr and Tywyn and the Korean news has increased its importance.

The report concludes with: 'When is the row going to start? We need one.' We see below that the 'row' starts with Plaid Cymru taking a leading role in the issue.

Abhorrent Profanity that Prostituted the Vale

We have seen, above, the efforts of the War Department to extend the land for technical firing reasons, i.e. that the latest shells could reach further, and in terms of safety in relation to the wider area of the shell burst in the danger area. It was also noted that this had led to a public inquiry in Dolgellau and that the residents of the area had strong feelings against the scheme. We will appreciate a little more of the feelings of the people at the time in this part that led to a series of protests being organised by Plaid Cymru against the proposed extension.

It has already been noted that no great sympathy had existed between the community and the military, and this is clearly seen in a short essay entitled 'Big Guns at Trawsfynydd' by Dyfnallt, (Rev. John Dyfnallt Owen, 7 April 1873–28 December 1956, a Welsh poet, who also served as Archdruid of the National Eisteddfod of Wales):

In the last Days of July, 1914, I was on a brief visit to Hedd Wyn's neighbourhood. After an evening service, followed by some fascinating and joyful conversation and then a peaceful night at Blaenlliw, I was down-hearted on the morning to hear the thundering of the big guns from the vicinity of Trawsfynydd, and even more to my horror seeing the shells falling in the Feidiogydd area; and when I came across the ruins of the old sacred walls, my blood boiled with anger. The following day the first shots of the big guns were fired near the old chapel of Pen-y-Stryd; and so fierce were the blasts, that the windows were

Another civilian employed by the army was Robert Roberts; he can be seen here in the Camp's powerhouse

shattered, and the walls were damaged ... That night when I recounted the story of the destruction in Traws, there was a wild look in Hedd Wyn's eyes; and nobody was more outspoken against the abhorrent profanity that prostituted the vale than he was. In three years to the day he also fell in sacrifice to the same ravaging spirit.

To Shrewsbury

At the Parish meeting held on 15th January, 1948, the clerk read the notice calling the 'Parish Meeting' to consider the War Office's request for further land to practice at Trawsfynydd, on the south and east side of the existing camp. According to the record, 10,000 more acres had been requested in addition to the 8,000 they had at present. J. Ellis Hughes (Chair of the Parish Council) explained how much he knew about the situation, with E.M. Jones, the clerk, elaborating a little more and adding that he had a lot of correspondence with the War Office and the Town and Country Planning Department and that he understood that there was no certainty about the place at this time.

1. *Rev. Robert Davies (rear) and his family;*
2. *Councillor Daniel Jones*

This was followed up with heated debate. With the farmers naturally quite worried about their homes on the one hand, and those who worked in the camp on the other hand were anxious about their future, expressing concern that the camp would close down. As a result of the arguments for and against, it was decided to defer any decision until after the 'Shrewsbury Conference', on the 22nd of January 1948. Therefore, it was passed that three Members were to go to Shrewsbury, if they could attend, to listen and try to understand the matter and return with a report to the Parish Meeting. The Chairman was named, also Mr E.V. Pugh, Mr Daniel Jones and Rev. Robert Davies as a delegation, which is four people rather than three. After a vote the clerk suggested that it was appropriate to send the four that had been named, as the number of votes was very close between them.

By the Parish Meeting of the 19th of February 1948, the delegation had returned with a full report from the Conference, which was under the presidency of Emanuel 'Manny' Shinwell, who was the then Secretary of State for War.

Rev. Robert Davies was the first to report, saying that he had been to 'Shrewsbury and that it was a nice day, and there were from 40 to 50 in number present and that he had fallen in love with Shinwell, and that he said that there must be an army and one that was trained, or it would be of no value, and he did not see them as asking for no good land, and believed that they would be given every fair play by Mr Shinwell.'

The next to report was Mr E.V. Pugh. He felt the same as Mr Davies and also believed that they would have every fair play from Mr Shinwell.

However, the next one to report, Mr Daniel Jones was not of the same opinion. The conference did not wish to acknowledge that 'Wales has any distinctive characteristics, culture, or language, and that it provides much more training land from Wales than from England and Scotland.' The chair added facts about the land area used for practice by explaining that 1% of England, around 2% of Wales and less than 1% of Scotland was utilized.

The Parish Meeting's minutes note the concern of Mr David Tudor regarding the fact that none of the delegation had been allowed to speak at the conference, and asked the clerk to read out his letter which gave them permission to go there as listeners only. The only person to have said a word was Mr Emrys Roberts M.P.

The clerk went on to explain the size of the new 'Range', namely, 'from Ganllwyd up through Hafod Fraith and Tyddyn Mawr, Llanfachreth, and close to Rhyd y Gorlan school, and back to Brynllin and Twrmaen and Blaenlliw past Moel Llyfnant for Trinant and Llyn Tryweryn and Cwm Prysor Station and down to Darngae.' But Mr. Shinwell had said he was prepared to, 'give consideration and willing to consult with the local authorities, and if there was a special issue then an inquiry would have to be conducted.'

The record concludes with, 'Gratitude was expressed by Mr. Jacob Davies that the Members went to Shrewsbury and in

Front and back covers of Plaid Cymru's pamphlet objecting to extending the Ranges

particular to Mr. Tudor and Mr. Pugh for providing their vehicles free of charge for the Parish's service.'

There is no mention if the Parish Council was in favour or against the development. But it is interesting to note Mr Daniel Jones' points and to try to speculate from them what the motive and attitude of the Conference was towards Wales.

Defence Committee

'Wales Must Live', that was the message from Plaid Cymru's Meirion Committee campaign leaflet against extending the firing range. The front cover shows a photo of shells firing at night with the face of Clement Atlee as the face of the moon and the statue of Hedd Wyn as a disappointed spirit looking at the scene. Under the picture is an adaptation of 'Atgo' by Hedd Wyn (roughly translated as follows):

> None of our purple Moon
> Lights the mountain bare.
> But the sound of Atlee's shells
> Whizzing through the air.

Here's the remainder of the committee's message:

> The County of Meirion Committee has from the outset stood firm against the intentions of the War Office to take possession of the land of Meirion for the purpose of military exercises.
>
> We rejoice that a defence committee has been set up, representing every aspect of life in the county. We are privileged to work with this Committee to protect the highest values in society. We are firmly of the view that acquiring these Welsh areas, with their intrinsic culture, both socially and religiously – would mean the demise, not only of the community culture and agriculture, but also the soul of a nation.
>
> We believe that the special contribution of Wales to the world is the promotion of peace in the midst of nations, and that the extension of military camps in its land is an obstacle to this ideal.
>
> We will endeavour our utmost for our children to keep these areas as their heritage.

Gwynfor Evans' Encouragement

Gwynfor Evans as party president gave his support to the campaign by trying to inspire the farmers through his encouragement:

> Farmers of Meirion! Once again, the eyes of Wales look towards you, heirs and conservators of its rich culture and age-old traditions. We turn to you sympathetically because an alien government tries to steal from you

home and field and hill to feed the greed of militarists. But we also turn with confidence to the sons of Meirion who have always shown hatred for oppression and love for their homeland. I know that you stand firm and in line as you have always stood, challenging the Offices of the Warmongers to do their worst. In making a stance for home and for the community you will stand up for the country and the nation, and the influence of your example will be seen in a new loyalty for Wales.

The War Office had its way in Epynt. There, four hundred Welsh people were turned out of their farms, and today where there were homes now only stones remain, and the Welsh language was excluded from a beautiful and spacious area by the thunder of guns. But if Epynt was lost, we insist that no other area within it will be 'Epyntised'.

Protesters including Gwynfor Evans in 1951

Yours on Behalf of Wales,
Gwynfor Evans

'Do not give in'

D.J. Williams, Fishguard, also wrote to farmers in Meirion on the 20th of May, 1948:

Don't give in – we've won in Preseli ....

A year and a half ago the War Office threatened to occupy 16,000 acres of the land of Preseli for military purposes.

This oppression invoked the justified anger of all the inhabitants. Protests were immediately arranged, together with the formation of a defence committee and fund. In no time at all this fund was a thousand pounds. But as good as all this was, that is not what saved Preseli – but a strong, unmistakable statement from many of the residents, including three or four ministers of religion, who would not be moved from their homes if it came to the worst, lest they were dragged out of them by Government servants. The people of Wales own Wales, say the men of Preseli; and we have no right to surrender one piece of it to any alien Power.

War Office – too much of Meirion's Land

'I stand unshaken' were the words of John Jones, Brynllin, Abergeirw, going on to say:

I have spent close to sixty years of my life in this mountainous area, and my family were here before me. My roots are here. I learned to worship God in Abergeirw's ancient little chapel. I watched the increase in rural culture in the area, and I did what I could to promote it. A carefully cultivated 'Vineyard', will it be stampeded by pigs? I witnessed the destruction of Cwm Dolgain, and the scattering of its residents – good farmhouses used as road stones, the fields full of shell

Gwynfor Evans addressing the protesters

holes – the War Office already has TOO MUCH land.

I am determined that militarists and vandals will not destroy another valley of this old county – I stand unshaken.

Our Duty to Our Children

This is the view of Gwladys Roberts, Headmistress, Ysgol Rhydygorlan, Abergeirw:

Yes, our duty to the children of Ysgol Rhydygorlan – children brought up in homes that keep alive the best things in Welsh culture and are taught in a school that has the foundation of its education plan based upon that culture.

It is a fascinating place to have a school. Children respond to a teacher's effort, with the parents in the community behind every effort, and they work with the teacher in appreciating the things that have real value. It is refreshing to be in a school whose influence does not have to compete with the influence of the cinema, and where imitating gun fire is not counted as the main attraction of the playground. The children are well aware of the sound of the big guns, and there is something very repugnant about having to teach the principles of peace to small children in the midst of war preparations.

The people of Abergeirw have already stated clearly and unambiguously what their attitude to war is and we will not recognise that any government has the right to misuse ONE INCH of Welsh soil to teach men to kill each other.

That was the background of the community's feelings, a close and culturally rich community that was now ready to resist the might of the British Empire, and the background behind Plaid Cymru's campaign against extending the firing range. We'll now look at the protests that occurred during that campaign.

Gandhi's Non-violent Method

On Thursday morning of the 6th of September, 1951 at nine thirty, seventy-five protesters split into two groups in order to

Protesters near Pont Abergeirw

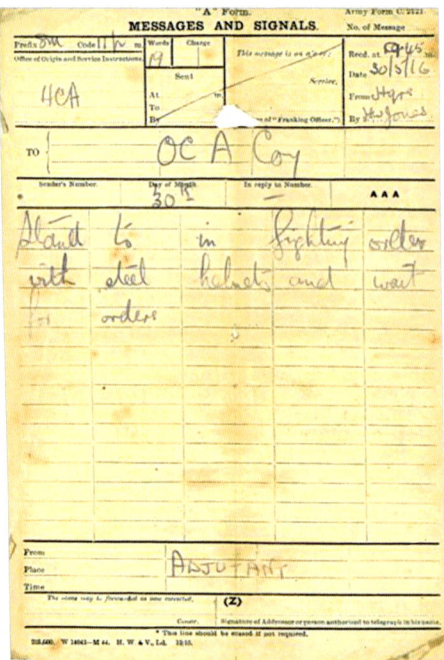

Example of a military order

sit on the road each end of the military Camp. One group sat near Bronaber on the western entrance, while the other group established themselves not far from Rhiwgoch at the eastern entrance.

Before they prepared themselves to sit,

Gwynfor Evans had earlier had a word with the protesters on how to behave. He appealed to them to be decent, polite, thoughtful and quiet in the face of any attempt to move them. And it was this regime they adopted throughout the protest, Gandhi's non-violent way of opposing. It is interesting to note that this was the first time that this method of protest was used in Wales. Although this was a Plaid campaign, it is also interesting to note that Gwynfor Evans said in his address that this was not a party act, but that each one was responsible for his own self and acted as individuals.

The objectors felt that all other means of declaring the dissatisfaction of the local and wider community had been ignored by the War Office. As noted before, there had been protests against the plan to extend the firing range at the public inquiry in Dolgellau in 1950. Also, previously at a conference of MPs (and others) in Llandrindod Wells in 1947, where there had been unanimous opposition against the idea. So, there was nothing for it but to show their opposition in an active way. A statement was shared out to the soldiers and other observers explaining the rationale behind the struggle against the occupation of more land at Trawsfynydd, explaining that all other democratic ways had failed. The statement went on to say: 'We must object in deed and in a word, such as our ancestors did before us ... we have no unkind feeling to the residents of the camp, be they officers, soldiers or workers, but only to the alien Government who introduced the aggression.'

Order to Drive Through

Things became agitated a couple of times during the day with vehicles trying to drive through the objectors. One of the workers at the camp drove his vehicle towards the crowd on the outskirts of Bronaber, pushing Dr Pennar Davies and Mr Glyn

Rhys Williams y Gors' shell collection

Jones and others, for several yards before turning back. Then, under an order from a young officer to drive through the protesters, one of the army trucks came there. The lorry pushed a number in front of it, including Gwynfor Evans and Mr Dan Thomas, before also stopping.

However, the crowd allowed some vehicles to pass through, such as the Meirion Creamery dairy lorry, livestock lorry, doctor and food and clothing transport vehicles.

The police came there around the middle of the day, five officers, Ffestiniog's Inspector and Chief Constable Williams. The protesters refused to move when asked and consequently their names were taken. However, the police showed goodwill and courtesy towards the protesters and once they had a word with the Camp's Commanding Officer, it was decided to allow the two groups to remain in their place until the end of the afternoon. As a result of the courtesy shown by the police, and as a gesture of gratitude, the protesters abandoned the protest an hour earlier than scheduled. They arose and walked from the camp in an orderly manner at four o'clock.

Letter to the Commanding Officer

The protesters also delivered a letter to the Commanding Officer on the day, this is its content:

Our act today is to symbolize the act of forming an obstacle to prevent the movement of vehicles into and out of Trawsfynydd camp; we hold the strong conviction that the War Office, in commandeering five thousand more acres for this camp, is destroying the heritage of the Welsh nation. The united conviction of the people of this county and of Wales as a whole was ignored despite being highlighted in every possible way, at a public inquiry and by other means. It showed that all the Government's claims that it is acting democratically in its dealings with Wales are empty gestures. The choice for us, as such, is to accept in a cowardly manner this further injustice on Wales or to oppose it in a more reactive way. We choose the second route because it is compatible with

1. Former military garage a storehouse and workshop now; 2. Former shower block; 3. Soldiers' former meat store

self-esteem and determination to keep Wales alive despite unsympathetic government aggression.

The impact of the occupation of this additional land in the centre of one of the most cultured and Welsh areas of our country would be detrimental. This part of Meirionnydd is one of the strongest sources of the Welsh way of life. It is a sinful act to occupy these lands and demolish the communities that have been living on them for centuries; and we are obliged to oppose that. The taking of the lands is a damaging operation, and it's ironic that it is legitimized in the name of defence. What defence does the Government require that causes the destruction of Wales? Wales did not will this devastation.

We wish to emphasise that in our actions today we have no unkind feeling to you or those under your command. We realise that you are only servants of a higher Authority, and Wales needs to oppose and change the policy of that Authority. The government heard the appeal of the Welsh nation to live its own special life and dismissed that appeal here in Meirionnydd and in various other counties in Wales. That is the aggression on our heritage that we oppose through non-violence.

Second Protest

The Saturday morning of the 29th September was a lovely morning with the sun illuminating the mountainous terrain and a blanket of mist shrouding the lake. It was a view confirming the protesters decision that this was a justified demonstration to save such a beautiful area from the horrors of military use.

The crowd started from Abergeirw early in the morning with their banners gleaming in the sun's golden hour that follows the dawn. Someone brought out a spade and dug a hole in the marshy land nearby to put the Red Dragon flag on a pole there. It was there that the crowd gathered around Gwynfor Evans to listen to his address:

We stand here today as representatives of a nation. That nation is being destroyed because it does not have a government that is seeking to protect and develop its life. It is an English government and the extent of that concern about Wales is seen in its attitude towards its land and the communities that live on it. Through various means, such as the War Office and the Forestry Commission, Welsh land is being stolen from under its feet, and in area after area we see the destruction of the Welsh way of life.

The classic example is Epynt where four hundred Welsh families were thrown out of their homes. Despite knowing that the impact of this avarice, and the massive camps that are placed in the heart of communities which have already been shaken, it is so much worse in Wales than in England yet more land is occupied on average in our own country than in England. And it is taken against the will of the Welsh people: the farce of a public inquiry in Dolgellau is testament to that.

We say that we cannot bend to this manifestation of undemocratic viciousness on Welsh opinion and life. We come here to claim that this land is the land of our country and that the offices of the English government have no moral right to it. We come to show the will of the Welsh people that the English government will not spoil our localities as easily as it may think. We do not come to injure or kill any person at all; unlike the War Office that we oppose, so it is not those methods that we use.

But we come in the knowledge that we are violating the law of the land by being here. In standing on this land, and in walking over it, we become criminals against that law. We know that, and we are prepared to accept the consequences. We previously breached the law a month ago. We have not been persecuted so far. That can be taken as an encouraging sign that the authorities regard Welsh nationalism as a force, and that they do not wish to strengthen it.

We plant the Welsh flag here. We will leave it here afterwards as a clear sign that this is the soil of Wales. The English government may not see the red flag flying here. The red flag has a greater significance. But the element of common danger is shared between them. The fact that the red flag waves above such ground is a sign of lethal danger to the Welsh nation.

*The late Evan Tudor in the front looking
towards the camera*

Danger Farm

With these inspiring words then resounding in the minds of the crowd, Llwyd o'r Bryn lead them in singing 'Land of my Fathers' before they returned to their cars.

Onward to the Camp

They started in one long row of cars on their way from Abergeirw through the firing range, but they were blocked by the vehicle of Lieutenant-colonel Jones Williams, the chief constable of Gwynedd. A small delegation, consisting of Gwynfor Evans and J.E. Jones, went to have a word with him. As before, the Chief Constable was ever courteous and polite to them. They chatted about a number of things including the weather before coming to the heart of the issue. He was given words of comfort by assuring him that they had no plans to damage or harm anyone in the camp. He was pleased with this and led them forward up to the Penstryd chapel, where they left their cars so that they could form a procession into the camp.

Just after they reached the entrance to the camp and sat down, a small van came towards them from the camp. The driver stopped before reaching them and explained that he needed to go to the bank before midday in order to change his wages cheque. Gwynfor Evans agreed to let him get through – but a larger van came along the road towards them at the same time. This was a bit of a dilemma for the protesters, that is, could the small van be allowed through without the larger one taking advantage of the gap and escaping through it? It was decided to retreat to one side only and leave only enough width for the small van to pass then close the line back swiftly to obstruct the other, and so it was.

'May I pass, Boss?' the driver asked Gwynfor Evans, and at the same time his companion offered a bag of biscuits from his pocket to the protesters. There was no response from the crowd, so after a few minutes the driver tried his luck again by saying, 'May I get through please, I want to meet my wife at midday.' But they wouldn't budge, so that he asked jokingly, 'Do they understand English?'

Shortly afterwards a commercial truck came from somewhere, and it was allowed to get through by opening only half the way as before and it went on – before the military van even fired its engine to try to seize the opportunity!

One more army van joined with the

other but did not make any difference to the protesters, including Gwynfor Evans, D.J. Williams, Fishguard, Dan Thomas and Llwyd o'r Bryn in the front row, who stared in a relaxed manner at the troops.

Before they got up at half past one the police officers came and took their names and addresses. Among the names collected were the four parliamentary candidates for Plaid Cymru: Dan Thomas (Wrexham), Wynne Samuel (Aberdar), Kitchener Davies (West Rhondda) and Rev. Eurwyn Morgan (Llanelli).

'I was just going to fetch a loaf!'

When researching the history of the demonstration I encountered a photograph of the protest near Bronaber. In the photograph is a young lad looking into the lens of the camera, he was the late Evan Tudor from the Aber farm not far from Bronaber. I asked Evan what his contribution was to the event and the answer I received was: 'Mam had asked me to go on an errand to the shop at the Camp. As I walked up the road from the Aber, a fleet of cars came towards me and those were full of protesters. They encouraged me to join, so I did – otherwise I was just going to fetch a loaf!'

I also questioned my Father about what he remembered; he was there at the time doing his national service. He remembered the first protest well, 'They were a bloody nuisance, we wanted to go to the dance in Portmadoc but they wouldn't let us through!' he said with a mischievous smile on his face.

Opinion of the Member of Parliament

This is a quote from the debate in Parliament from Hansard:

Mr George Thomas (Cardiff West): Am I mistaken in believing that my Hon. Friend was one of those people who laid down on a path to stop soldiers coming to Trawsfynydd?

Mr TW Jones: I am sure that my Hon. Friend does not wish to associate me with the acrobatic antics of the Welsh Nationalist Party. These people were not natives of Trawsfynydd. This afternoon I am speaking on behalf of the people of Trawsfynydd

Dôl Mynach Isa' Ford

Over:
Snow covered Ranges

Clearing the Ranges

The Camp became less important as a resource for the army as the fifties went on, and the place was closed as a military establishment for the last time in 1957-8, (but it reopened almost immediately to accommodate over 800 itinerant workers from other areas in order to build the Trawsfynydd nuclear power station).

Here's an extract from an article from the *Y Dydd* newspaper, January, 1958:

The clearing of bombs and bullets from the Trawsfynydd firing range will begin on January 7, at which time 120 soldiers from Crickhowell, Brecknockshire, will embark on two weeks of work there. Men from other units will follow them.

The land comprises some 8,700 acres owned by the Army and about another 2,200 acres claimed by the Army under Defence Rules. The whole range will be transferred back into civilian possession after the closure of the Army Practical Training Area. It was announced that the army was giving up the land in March 1958.

If enough troops are available it is planned to clear the land, where the army has rights to train and fire, by the end of 1958, and the rest by the spring of 1959.

The land is examined very carefully by teams of ten men and an officer. No men are allowed to work for more than forty minutes and cannot do this job for more than six weeks in a year.

Special equipment is used for those places where large numbers of shells are known to have fallen.

Bomb-making Memories

I remember when we were youths; we went up to the Ranges on our bikes to collect '303' rifle bullets with the intention of making 'bombs' with them. We knew where the locations of one or two of the 'ammunition dumps' were and there we would pick up the live bullets and put them in the bike's saddle bag. After we went home, the next task was to carefully remove the bullet from the cartridge to expose the cordite, the bit that made it go bang! There was considerable trial and error to see what would make the best 'bomb'; some cordite was placed in an empty 'Bovril' jar with a 'fuse' once, on the path leading to Cae Coch, near the village Rectory, which then exploded with pieces of glass scattering everywhere! While the experiment was a successful one in a sense, it was decided that it was too dangerous to try it again.

On another occasion, Llion Williams, Dei Rowlands and I went at it to try and make another type of 'bomb'. In the garden of Dei's parents' house in Cefn Gwyn, where we wrapped up layers of aluminium foil around the cordite, until it was about the size of a cricket ball. It was a lovely day and ideal for clothes drying in the light wind. We then made a camp fire in the style of boy scouts, a circle of stones at the top end of the garden, a bit of dry grass, with some twigs on it and some lumps of coal for good measure; we lit the fire and threw the 'ball' into it. We rushed into the house as soon as we could, where

303 Rifle Bullet

we crouched down and stared out of the living room window. After about a minute or two, there was a huge bang from the fire, with the twigs, turfs, and the lumps of coal shooting into the air before mushrooming some twenty feet up in the sky and falling on top of the clothes that were drying on the line – suffice to say that was the end of our bomb-making experiments!

Pig Bristle and its Stench!

A unique (and smelly!) industry came to Mynydd Bach above Cwm Dolgain in July 1967, by way of a site for the treatment of pig skins to obtain the bristle for paint brushes for the 'Harris Brushes' Company. The company used to have the bristle from China primarily since the 1930s, but they raised the price by 80% in the early sixties, so it was decided to process the skins themselves. The old army gun park was ideal to spread out the skins, so they could weather in the sun, wind and rain – a process that took two or three months, with the need to turn them with a fork on

Local rally driver, Ken Pugh, on the former Harris Brushes' pig bristle site

a weekly basis. After they were dried and odour-free they would be returned to the factory in Stoke Prior to be washed, straightened and graded before being installed in the brushes. With the advent of synthetic fibres, there was no need any longer to treat the bristle. So, the process came to an end after being on site for about nine years – something that was very much welcomed by the residents of the area as sometimes a few of the skins would fall off the lorries leaving the most terrible stench on the roadside.

The site is now owned by Bala Motor Club and there are rally time trials there two or three times a year.

The End?

But is this the end of the firing ranges' story? Not really, in January 2006 the National Park Authority decided to extend a prohibition to the public from having access to 250 acres of land in the firing area, and this was in order for contractors to have a two-year opportunity to get rid of the unexploded weapons of war. The length of time was clearly not enough, as can be seen from the warnings there today, the ban continues until the 26th of August 2023 – a hundred and twenty years since the first big guns were fired!

And what about the Camp? In 1969, the author's father, John ('O'B') O'Brien's construction company successfully won a contract from Cecil Williams, the site owner, to build Norwegian log cabins on the bases of former military buildings. So O'B came back to the Camp, the place where he did his national service nearly 20 years earlier, now building the cabins, employing up to 16 local men when the place was at its busiest, with 8 cabins arriving from Norway every two weeks in the early 70s. There was a lot of fun with Odd and Allan – two workers from Trondheim, Norway, who had come over to train them on how to erect the cabins. The Camp again played an important role in his life and employed some of his old friends from the military, such as John Thompson and Tommy Harrison and his

1. Exclusion sign; 2. John O'Brien, Gwyn Jones and Haydn Jones building the shop in the early 70's; 3. Llanfachreth Village Hall near Dolgellau – former Traws Camp building having a new lease of life after the camp closed. It is still in regular use.

Part of the former firing range in use by the army as part of the Vambrace Warrior exercise in Autumn 2016

other friend Hughie McMormick frequently driving a JCB for him. He was there for 27 years and developed a great friendship with the late David Day, later owner of the site. David also ventured to build a ski slope above Rhiwgoch, using the Camp's old drinking water reservoir as part of a unique misting system to make the ski mats feel more like snow.

To conclude this book, I feel it appropriate to quote extracts out of an essay by Beti Wyn Lloyd, formerly of Pantglas, at about the beginning of the '60s:

The valley's population was considerable before the troops came. Apart from the tenants and their families, a servant and maid were employed, if not more, at Hafodty Bach, Dol Mynach, Gwynfynydd, Bedd y Coedwr, Dolgain, Llech Idris and Dol Moch. Men with scythes would also come to Dolgain, Gwynfynydd, Llech Idris and Dolmynach. An employment fair was held to employ scythe-men in Trawsfynydd at this time and would always be well attended.

Almost invariably there was good singing in Penstryd chapel and the family of Edward Rowlands, Feidiog Bach were very melodious. The son, Dafydd Rowlands, moved to Dolgellau and successfully led the main choir there. It should be noted that his son, Dafydd Rowlands, led the similarly successful Dolgellau Male Choir. Owen Rowlands, Feidiog Bach, was also the father of the well-known singer Ted Rowlands, who also performed duets across Wales with Mr Moses Hughes, Fronwnion.

Then there was Huw Rowlands and Evan Jones, Defeidiog Isa' who sang duets often together. I heard about them going to a major eisteddfod in Bala and singing for Dr. Joseph Parry and winning, despite keen competition, and thus gaining great praise for themselves. But I heard Huw Rowlands, Tyngriafolen, acknowledging that Ellis Jones, Defeidiog, was the champion when he competed. He rarely sang, but he said he had an excellent and unbeatable voice.

It must also be remembered that the late William Jones, Hafodwen, won many awards including the Blue Ribbon at the National Eisteddfod, a son of Annie Jones, formerly of Gelligain. He had his roots firmly in Cwm Dolgain.

In this period, the boundaries were stone walls, and the sons of Defeidiog Bach were very masterful in the art of so-called dry wall construction.

I also remember that there would be a ploughing churn there – the only one in the vicinity, and it was consistently used for churning.

Shepherding and Shearing

The residents of the valley were always considered as good shepherds. On an open mountain one needed sharpness to identify and sort the sheep, and everyone was very honest and sincere in this direction. Everyone would help each other to cut peat, and also on shearing day. That was a very important and interesting day. There had to be a shearing competition for lambs in every farm, and Wmffra Jones, Hafodty Bach would organise the contest with much fun and humour. Fairly weak shearers would come from Waen y Bala, Cwm Parc and Cefnddwysarn, but they, too, soon learned much and improved.

The Smithy

The Smithy at Penstryd was a very important place at this time, and folk from Cwm Prysor, the Ganllwyd Valley and Cefn Clawdd would come there to shoe horses and cattle. Robin Go' (the blacksmith) would walk to Kent and other places in England with the cows, taking his horseshoes and cattle shoes or clips with him to shoe on the journey. He was a big, muscular man, but extremely kind to birds and animals. The little birds would land on his head and shoulders, and he would never kill a little mouse, but instead release it and tell it not to come back!

He could also fight, but only needed to hit his enemy once – since that person would barely be able get up after! He could speak five languages – Latin, Greek and French, as well as English and Welsh. He died in 1902 and was buried in the cemetery of Penstryd.

That's a brief overview of things like they were in Cwm Dolgain before 1903. That was the year that the troops came to Bryn Golau, Trawsfynydd, and started practicing in Cwm Dolgain.

The Arrival of the Soldiers

As might be expected there had been considerable change in the valley, but no-one had to leave their farm up to two years later. Instead, everyone had to move during the day from about eight in the morning to seven or eight in the evening to tents. The tents of Feidiog Bach were at the top of the Feidiog on Blaenlliw Mountain; the Dol Moch and Hafod y Garreg tents at the top of Llechwedd Cain at the Nant y Frwydr boundary. The tents of Feidiog Isa', Gelli Gain and Llech Idris were at Penstryd, and those of Dol Mynach Ucha' at Dol Mynach Isa'. Everyone had to wait in their tents until the soldiers had finished firing. This meant that they had to

1. Glynda O'Brien at Foty Llelo, her great-grandfather's home; 2. William Williams, Brynllefrith at Dôl Mynach Isa'; 3. Buarth Brwynog fireplace

stay late in the shelters, and this made it very difficult for the farmers to cultivate the land and collect the harvest.

They would get up with the dawn to cut and cultivate the hay and then again in the late evening. But despite everything, everyone got his crop by the end of the summer. The Defeidiog Isa' family would send their cattle to Gelli Gain during the day in order to be safe from the firing.

In 1905 the soldiers moved from Bryn Golau to Rhiwgoch and the tenants were given notice to quit, despite having nowhere to go. The family of Defeidiog Bach moved to the Chapel House, Cwm Prysor. Dol Moch's family went to Gilfach Wen and the families of Hafod y Garreg and Defeidiog Isa' to Nant y Frwydr, one family in the parlour and the other in the kitchen. The Dol Mynach family went to Brynllefrith and the Gelli Gain family went to Bedd y Coedwr. The family of Llech Idris were fortunate to have Bryn Golau. No other residents of the valley were forced to move.

Break-up

After this break-up the congregation of Penstryd Chapel decreased, but the cause continued there.

There were many who got work in the camp building roads and similar things. This continued throughout the time the troops were there.

The tenants of Defeidiog Isa' had been the shepherds of Morus Evans over the years, and when those named moved from the valley he became the tenant of their farms, Defeidiog Isa', part of Brynllin Fawr, Dol Mynach Isa', Dol Mynach Ucha', Llech Idris, Dolgain and Gelli Gain. After that only the shepherds of Morus Evans lived at Dolgain. The old farms were left to deteriorate until they were ruins. The verse (roughly translated) discovered on the lintel above the doorway at Hafodty Plas * (Foty Llelo) could easily be repeated whilst gazing at each of them:

Many a spring smiled evermore
In turquoise at your door;
Time's fingerprints so meek
Are carved upon your cheek

Field telephone box near Gelli Gain

* Note: The grandfather of Glynda (author's wife), Owen Thomas Jones 'Now Tom' was born at Foty Llelo. He lost his eye in the early days of the Battle of the Somme in 1916, also his brother Ellis John was killed at the Battle of Passchendaele on the 27th of August 1917, almost exactly a month after Hedd Wyn.

The Valley after the Soldiers Left

When the soldiers departed there was a very different look to Cwm Dolgain. There was nothing but bare land with scars and rushes, all in an endless mix along its length. Very few of the old farms were left – only some stones and a few trees to mark the spot.

The tenants had the opportunity to buy back the farms. Evan Jones Pantglas had his mountain pasture and Rhiwgoch. Dol Moch went back to Huw Rowlands and Bryngath mountain pasture to Daniel Roberts. John Jones, Bronaber also bought Hafodty Bach. The old tenancy of Morus Evans was divided – Dol Mynach Isa' and Dol Mynach Ucha to D.M. Davies, Ty Cerrig, Bala Park, and Defeidiog Isa', Dolgain, Llech Idris and Gelli Gain to Bryn Davies, Pant Neuadd, Y Parc.

The Forestry Commission took part of Defeidiog Isa' and Defeidiog Bach, and now only trees are seen on the land.

A new house was built in Dolgain and they started farming the land again there and at Dol Mynach.

The road was rebuilt over to the Blaenlliw Valley and you can now travel in a motorcar up Cwm Dolgain, but we observe in passing that there is (roughly translated):

> No smoke in Buarth Brwynog,
>   No song at Gelli Gain,
> Nor nothing at Foty Llelo
>   But crows' nests in the pine.
>
> Silence at Dol Mynach,
>   Llech Idris with no door ajar,
> Dei went away from the Feidiog,
>   There's nothing there but a scar.
>
> In Hafod Garreg ruins,
>   And Nant Llwcus shattered,
> The old society decimated
>   And to the four winds scattered.

1. Penstryd Observatory;
2. Arthur Rowlands indicating location of Dôl Moch Splinter Shelter

Danger Farm

And whilst gleaming waves
    Pervade the river Cain and its flow
There will be a longing in my heart
    For the valley I once did know.

1. Field telephone box between Penstryd Chapel and Dolgain; 2. Bunker adjacent to the Anti-tank Range near the ruins of Gelli Gain; 3. Big guns being drawn through Bronaber or "Tin Town" as it was known

Acknowledgments

The late Eirianwen John (my grandmother) for her memories of soldiers' laundry at Stryd Faen;

Gwilym Williams, Bryn Llefrith, for the history of the Feidiog Isa' tragedy out of a copy of the *Y Faner*, 1882;

The late Isgoed Williams, Trawsfynydd for his memories of horse movements at the Camp;

Gareth Dafydd, formerly of Trawsfynydd, for a copy of the deeds of the Cwm Dolgain lands; Giovanna Bloor, Croesor for information about 'K Force';

The late R. Gareth Williams, Trawsfynydd for his memories of keeping sheep on the Ranges;

Mrs Glenys Cartwright for a copy of her father, H.W. Jones' 'Fighting Orders';

Enid Williams, Llan Ffestiniog for the photo of her father in front of Rhiwgoch's front door;

Willie Pirrie for old photos of the Camp;

Margaret Jones, Ffriddbryncoch, for old photos of Rhiwgoch;

Dan Jones, Beaumaris, for the photo of his father, Daniel Jones;

Dylan Davies, Parc, Y Bala, for the photo of Dolmynach Isa';

Margaret Roberts for her late father-in-law's photo, Robert Roberts (Bob Dolau);

Ieuan Tomos, Llawplwy', for discovering the balloon's history and handing it to me;

Gwilym H. Jones for providing a copy of Plaid Cymru's campaign pamphlet and the photograph of the protesters at Abergeirw;

The late Evan Tudor, Yr Aber, Bronaber, and my late father, John O'Brien for their memories of the protest.

Rhys Williams and his family, Y Gors, Cwm Prysor, for their warm welcome and willingness to show the military remains on his land.

Similarly, for my brother-in-law, Arthur Rowlands and his loyal bitch Siân, for taking me on the quad bike to see the remains on Dol Moch mountain pasture – an experience and a half!

John Roberts, Snowdonia National Park's Archaeologist, for his interest and willingness to assist;

Ifan Gwyn Jones, Llanelltyd, for the drone view photo of Rhiwgoch following the fire;

Glynda O'Brien, my wife, and Julie Anne Rowlands, my sister, for their invaluable help in proof-reading the book's draft manuscript;

And last but not least, Dwynwen Williams

from Gwasg Carreg Gwalch for her patience and professional help in editing the book.

Note: This book is an English translation and slight update of the original Welsh version *Maes y Magnelau* published by Gwasg Carreg Gwalch in 2018.

Willie Pirrie in front of a Bedford MW in the 1950's

Bibliography

Otterburn Training Area Then and Now, Defence Estates

Bala Junction to Blaenau Festiniog, D.W. Southern

A History of Trawsfynydd, Merched y Wawr and Traws-Newid (2012)

Meirionnydd Archives Documents, Gwynedd Council

History of the Army Service Corps (1939 – 1946), Brig. V.J. Moharir, AVSM (Retd.)

The Times, 13 June, 1930

Trawsfynydd Artillery Range Bye Laws 1941, HMSO

The Life of Samuel Franklin Cody, Jean Roberts

Daily Post, 18 November, 1949

Cambrian News, 14 July, 1950

Rhamant a Rhyddid [Romance and Freedom]: 'Hedd Wyn', J. Dyfnallt Owen (1952)

Protest pamphlet, Meirion Committee, Plaid Cymru (1948)

Y Cymro (7 September and 5 October, 1951)

Y Dydd (January 1958)

1. and 2. Llechweddgain Observatory before and after renovation, through the assistance of Snowdonia National Park Authority

cerddi'r Bugail

Hedd Wyn
(Ellis H. Evans 1887-1917)
cyflwyniad gan Gruffudd Antur

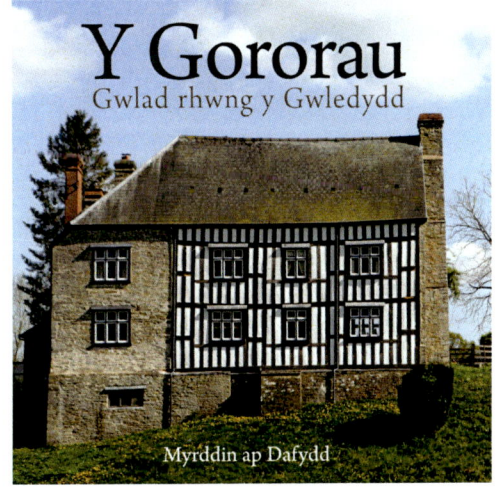

Y Gororau
Gwlad rhwng y Gwledydd

Myrddin ap Dafydd

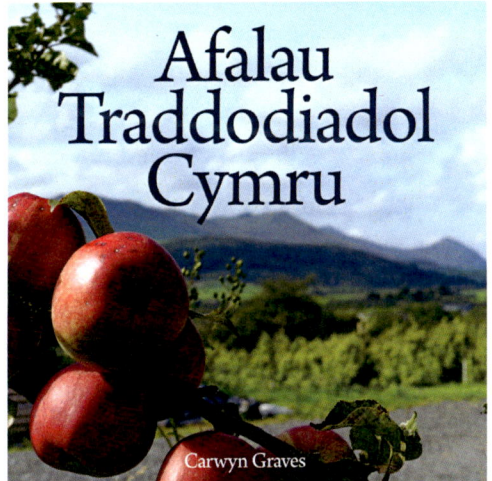

Afalau Traddodiadol Cymru

Carwyn Graves

Sbrigyn o Gelyn Coch

WILLIAM OWEN

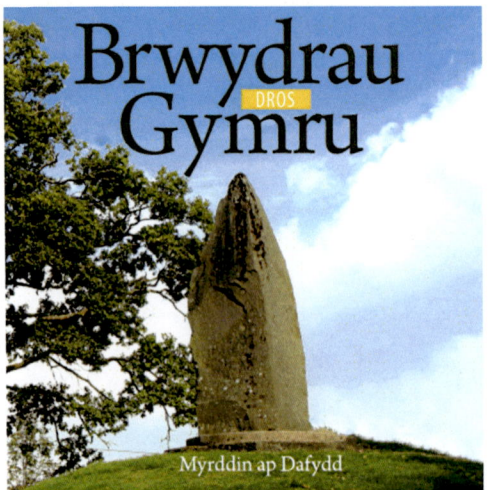

Brwydrau DROS Gymru

Myrddin ap Dafydd

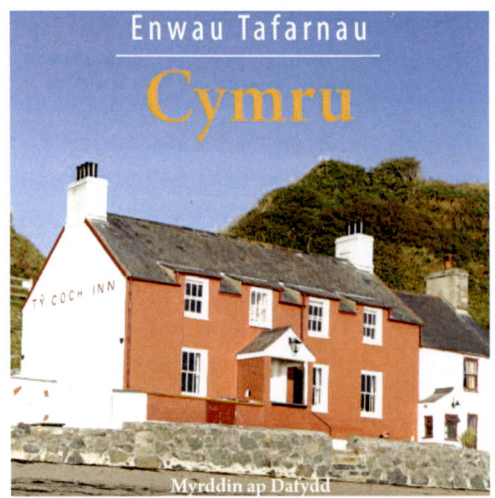

Enwau Tafarnau

Cymru

TŶ COCH INN

Myrddin ap Dafydd

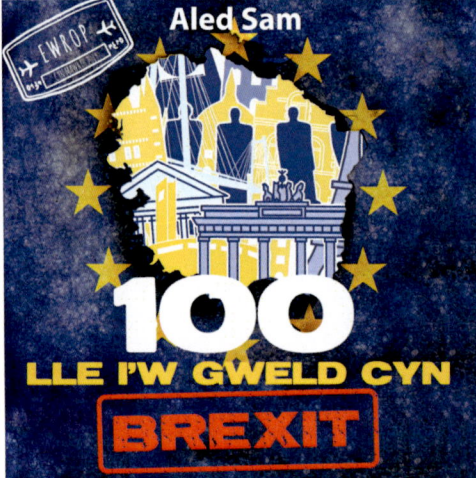

Aled Sam

EWROP

100
LLE I'W GWELD CYN
BREXIT

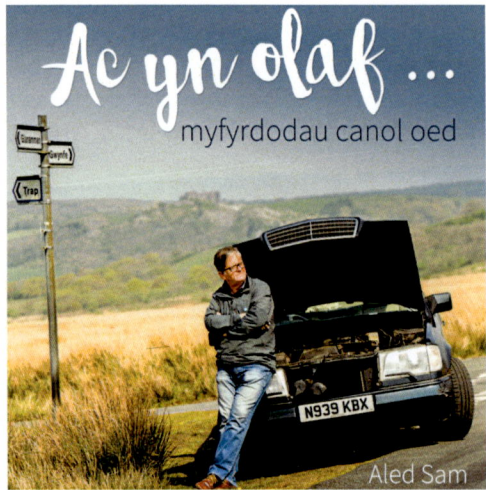

Ac yn olaf ...
myfyrdodau canol oed

Aled Sam